Transcultural Counselling in Action

SAGE Counselling in Action
Series Editor: Windy Dryden

SAGE Counselling in Action is a bestselling series of short, practical introductions designed for students and trainees. Covering theory and practice, the books are core texts for many courses, both in counselling and other professions such as nursing, social work and teaching. To celebrate its 20th Anniversary, SAGE has redesigned the series with a fresh, contemporary look to re-launch it into its next 20 years of widespread readership and success. Books in the series include:

Windy Dryden and Andrew Reeves
Key Issues for Counselling in Action

Dave Mearns and Brian Thorne
Person-Centred Counselling in Action, Third Edition

Ian Stewart
Transactional Analysis Counselling in Action, Third Edition

Peter Trower, Andrew Casey and Windy Dryden
Cognitive-Behavioural Counselling in Action, Second Edition

Tim Bond
Standards and Ethics for Counselling in Action, Second Edition

Sue Culley and Tim Bond
Integrative Counselling Skills in Action, Second Edition

Windy Dryden
Rational Emotive Behavioural Counselling in Action, Third Edition

Michael Jacobs
Psychodynamic Counselling in Action, Third Edition

Petrūska Clarkson
Gestalt Counselling in Action, Third Edition

Transcultural Counselling in Action

2nd Edition

Patricia d'Ardenne and Aruna Mahtani

Los Angeles • London • New Delhi • Singapore • Washington DC

Patricia d'Ardenne and Aruna Mahtani 1999

First published 1989
Reprinted 1990, 1991, 1992, 1993, 1994, 1996, 1998
Second Edition published 1999
Reprinted 2002, 2003, 2004, 2008

SAGE Publications Ltd
1 Oliver's Yard
55 City Road
London EC1Y 1SP

SAGE Publications Inc.
2455 Teller Road
Thousand Oaks, California 91320

SAGE Publications India Pvt Ltd
B 1/I 1 Mohan Cooperative Industrial Area
Mathura Road
New Delhi 110 044

SAGE Publications Asia-Pacific Pte Ltd
33 Pekin Street #02-01
Far East Square
Singapore 048763

Library of Congress Control Number available

British Library Cataloguing in Publication data

A catalogue record for this book is available from the British Library

ISBN 978-0-7619-6314-1
ISBN 978-0-7619-6315-8 (pbk)

Typeset by M Rules
Printed in Great Britain by The Cromwell Press, Trowbridge, Wiltshire
Printed on paper from sustainable resources

To Alistair Berkley.
Killed at Lockerbie

CONTENTS

Foreword to the Second Edition

'Let me not to the marriage of true minds admit impediment.' But, if the two minds attempting to marry are those of professional counsellor and his or her clients the impediments can seem insurmountable. Class is an obvious difficulty. But culture and race are potentially the biggest and most intractable barrier of all.

This is not an easy issue. It is relatively simple to grasp some practical details about somebody else's culture, but it is a huge and complex task to get white mental health professionals to come to terms with how racism mediates their relationship with their non-white clients. Academic research, into matters like the disproportionate numbers of black people diagnosed as schizophrenic, has begun to shed light on how racism and cultural prejudice have affected the treatment mental health professionals dish out to black people.

Even within a family there can be a gulf of understanding. And as a black child growing up in London in the 1960s I was baffled by the frequency and the poignancy of my father's complaints that I and my brother had no 'respect'. It took thirty years and the chance to visit and observe the rural Jamaica where he grew up for it to dawn on me what cultural and social resonance the word had for him. And why it mattered.

In practice most counselling of black people in Britain is 'transcultural'. This book is a clear and painstaking attempt to raise the issues of cultural and racial bias and offer guidelines and a model of good practice. Above all, it places the responsibility for good transcultural practice on the counsellors from the dominant culture.

Ideally there should be many more black professionals in the field and black people should have the choice of being counselled by someone of their own culture. Sadly, in the ten years since I wrote the Foreword to the first edition of this book there has been relatively little progress in empowering black people in the world of psychology and mental health, and the number of black counsellors remains far too low.

Diane Abbott, MP for Hackney North
House of Commons, London

PREFACE TO SECOND EDITION

It is ten years since we were first commissioned to write *Transcultural Counselling in Action*. The book was an early attempt in the field of published work on counselling theory across cultures in the UK, and affirmed what many of our colleagues were already undertaking in practice. At the time 'racism' was considered to be both too confrontational and of a minority interest to readers. Although we accepted 'transcultural' in our title, we endeavoured to address the effects of racism within the text. We worked towards counselling the inner world of the client in the context of external political reality. Our professional lives have also developed in both domains. We were both founder members of the British Psychological Society's Special Interest Group on Clinical Psychology 'Race' and Culture – one of us was the founding Chair. We have assisted the BPS in producing relevant training for clinical psychologists, and continue to teach, train, and challenge practitioners in institutional settings.

The world has moved on. Or has it? At one level, there is more published work on 'race', culture and counselling. There is now a greater currency in these terms in counselling training and practice. The cultural climate at the end of the twentieth century is more focused on client choice and empowerment, in healthcare, social services and community settings. What is lacking, however, is a depth of understanding about the effects of racism beyond what is expedient and politically correct. In reality, few counselling organisations give a choice to their minority ethnic clients of a counsellor from a similar background. We have frequently heard it said that there are not enough trained black counsellors, with little reflection on why this might be, or what changes would be required by policy makers. Our opinion is that change will only happen if we all act more proactively, in a range of settings, such as career promotion in schools, training bilingual counsellors, and promoting anti-racism in the workplace. In the wider world, counsellors have a responsibility to advocate best practice for diverse communities.

PREFACE TO FIRST EDITION

We have each spent a good part of our lives out of our countries of origin, and our approach to counselling reflects these experiences. One of us co-founded a multicultural mental health service in Brussels, which gave her her first insights into transcultural work. The other has to deal continually with the anomalies of life in two very different continents and cultures. We have both lived and worked in parts of London that have several very large culturally different communities. Our clients here come from a wide range of countries and cultures, and our work with them has helped us appreciate the importance in counselling of life experiences and background.

By contrast, our formal and professional training as clinical psychologists has limited our ability to work across cultures. Our counselling skills were taught to us in order to consider those variables between ourselves and our clients which would promote relationships for change and growth. In practice, however, institutionalised racism has meant that cultural issues are rarely given importance, and are often minimised in the counselling relationship.

We have found that the commonly held view of 'counselling' contains assumptions that are popular in European and North American cultures. Individuality, emphasis on past events and the detachment of the counsellor are not universal priorities; they may be of little value to counsellors and clients who do not 'belong' to the majority culture. Ethnocentric counsellors tend to see cultural differences as deviations from norms that they consider as global. These counsellors also presume that any differences are intrinsic to the clients and problematic, rather than a reflection of cultural contrast. Counsellors fit their clients to existing resources rather than develop their skills in response to clients' cultural needs. This book challenges counsellors to use their own resources more flexibly, and to give clients more effective counselling across cultures.

Transcultural Counselling in Action is one of a series of books aimed at providing guidelines of good practice in counselling, and we hope that it will be useful to readers whatever their background or orientation. It is intended for those whose work brings them into contact with many different cultural communities, but we hope that a wider readership will be encouraged to consider these issues for all counselling training and development. We want the book to be useful to people who counsel at many levels, for example, teachers, community workers, health visitors, doctors, as well as mental health professionals.

Transcultural counselling has its origins in practice rather than theory. There remains little established methodology or well-documented research to refer to. By contrast, there are many texts on racism as well as a growing body of work on mental illness and race and culture. Anthropologists too have turned away from the 'exotic' and begun to focus on communities on their doorsteps, coping with the day-to-day demands of change, economic hardship and racism.

Counselling across cultures is a recent approach for many neglected client groups. The practices quoted in this book have come from community groups, liaison and advocacy workers, from professionals already working with other cultures, from voluntary mental health agencies and from professionals from the communities themselves. We have selected four clients for this book who demonstrate a range of cultural issues, and have outlined general principles of practice.

This book is not intended to be an encyclopaedia of all cultural requirements. The content would be very long, very varied and very quickly out of date.

Transcultural counselling is *not* about being an expert on any given culture, nor does it adhere to a particular school of counselling. Rather, it is a way of thinking about clients, where culture is acknowledged and valued. We believe that effective counsellors need this approach in their general repertoire if they are to hear and respond to the needs of *all* their clients.

On a personal note, we ourselves have learnt enormously about each other's cultures in writing this book. In working together, we have had to look long and hard at our own cultural assumptions and have then had to find a transcultural way forward.

Patricia d'Ardenne
Aruna Mahtani
London

1

INTRODUCING TRANSCULTURAL COUNSELLING

Counselling has been one of the growth industries in the last decade of the millennium. Counsellors have attempted to respond to the needs, beliefs and circumstances of the people that seek and use them. It is now over thirty years since Truax and Carkhuff (1967) published their definitive text, *Towards Effective Counseling and Psychotherapy*. Their index, however, contained no entries under 'culture', 'race', or 'ethnic origin'. A likely explanation for this omission is that a transcultural approach to counselling was not yet perceived to be significant enough for separate consideration. Few of the counselling needs of ethnic groups had been documented or described by those writing on and researching counselling methods. Truax and Carkhuff (1967) maintained that it was possible to be a 'good counsellor', to have genuineness, non-possessive warmth, and accurate and empathic understanding, without further embellishment. 'Good' counsellors were presumed to be effective with all their clients, whether within or between cultures.

Carl Rogers (1951), on the other hand, refers to the desirability of counselling students having some knowledge of clients within their cultural setting. Further, Rogers (1951: 437) observes, 'Such knowledge needs to be supplemented by experiences of living with or dealing with individuals who have been the product of cultural influences very different from those which have molded the student.' Although he does refer to culture in the context of counselling, Rogers (1951) does not examine this concept in any further detail, nor does he indicate the skills that counsellors use in practice.

The specific skills required for counselling culturally different clients have been significantly developed over the past two decades. We have written this book to describe the features that currently define effective counselling across cultures in a straightforward and practical way.

WHAT IS COUNSELLING?

There are as many different definitions of counselling as there are therapeutic approaches, but a common working model will be proposed and used. The British Association for Counselling (1985) which represents counselling at a national level in Britain, defines 'counselling' as:

> When a person, occupying regularly or temporarily the role of counsellor, offers or agrees explicitly to offer time, attention and respect to another person or persons temporarily in the role of client.

In our working model, counselling has many of the components of short-term psychotherapy, that is it is a relationship aimed at facilitating the process by which clients change their feelings understanding and behaviour. Our model is essentially client-centred and non-hierarchical.

By client-centred, we mean that clients and their significant others are the focus of the relationship and make the choices about change. Counsellors do not offer solutions; they offer a relationship where the client can safely look at personal difficulties and move towards change. Counsellors enable their clients to recognise and use their personal resources more effectively. By non-hierarchical we mean that *both* clients and counsellors have skills that will be used co-operatively in the counselling process. Our model of counselling places more emphasis on the relationship between counsellors and their clients than on the theoretical framework of individual counsellors.

Furthermore, we believe that effective counsellors are people who demonstrate the essential qualities of genuineness, non-possessive warmth and empathy with their clients. Counsellors treat their clients with non-judgemental respect, and hope to introduce practical ways in which this can be achieved across any cultural divide.

WHAT IS CULTURE?

The terms 'culture', 'ethnic groups' and 'race' are frequently used to express very different ideas about a society. Fernando (1991) has described a helpful framework for distinguishing between these terms, (Figure 1.1, see p. 13). Our search for the meaning of 'culture' has shown that many workers in the field have struggled to achieve a workable definition of it. Before we can consider the use of 'culture' in *our* practice, it is important to look at how others have used this term.

For example, Triandis (1980) includes both physical and subjective aspects in his definition of 'culture'. He quotes roads, buildings and tools as physical elements of culture, and myths, roles, values and attitudes as subjective ones. On the other hand, Reber (1985: 170) defines 'culture' as 'the system of information that codes the manner in which the people in an organised group, society or nation interact with their social or physical environment'. Reber also emphasises that 'culture' pertains only to *non-genetic* character-istics and that people must *learn* these systems and structures.

Different groups of people, such as anthropologists, psychiatrists or politicians, are able to use the term 'culture' for their own diverse pur-poses. Sashidharan (1986), for example, has observed that in psychiatry, words like 'culture' and 'ethnicity' are not neutral terms; instead these words take on a politically loaded meaning. Fernando (1988) endorses this view when he asserts that 'culture' is used in psychiatry in an ethno-centric way. Consequently, non-Western cultures that are alien to psychiatry are themselves seen as pathological In this way 'culture' becomes the 'problem' that accounts for the abnormal behaviour of the client. Lago and Thompson (1996) have extensively debated the com-plexity of 'culture', and what differences in culture might mean between counsellors and clients.

In talking about culture, we have found that people avoid the more emotive aspects of this term, for example, 'race' or 'class', because they fear being faced with their own deeply-held prejudices. We are dealing with a complex and value-laden topic.

In common use, the term 'culture' has come to mean any difference between one group of people and another. Some researchers refer to dif-ferences in family role, gender, lifestyle, religion or politics as 'cultural' differences. In fact the term covers a very wide range of issues to do with the way people live. For our purposes, therefore, *'culture' means the shared history, practices, beliefs and values of a racial, regional or religious group of people.*

In practice, this definition of culture requires that counsellors seeing clients from other cultures will consider the following:

A Shared History

A client from a particular cultural group has a common set of previous experiences that brings that group of people together and helps them to define who they are. For example, counsellors who see clients with a history of white oppression and colonialism appreciate the anger that this generates, their own response to that anger and the impact of this on the counselling relationship.

Religion

Clients from another culture will have ways in which their faith and worship define them and which prescribe moral purpose and practices for everyday living. For example, a counsellor seeing a Roman Catholic woman contemplating abortion would need to understand how her religious belief about the sanctity of unborn life will influence her thinking and feeling, and subsequent decision.

Family Values and Intimate Relationships

Individual societies have accepted beliefs and expressions of family life, including marriage and child rearing. For example, any counsellor dealing with a client from an Indian cultural background needs to be sensitive to the difference between Western individualist counselling and the client's collectivist culture. The counsellor understands the importance of family responsibility and respect for elders within this framework.

WHAT IS 'RACE'?

Science in the last two centuries has legitimised the concept of 'race' as a means of classifying human beings on the basis of biological characteristics. Research on 'race' 'was used to justify slavery, imperialism, anti-immigration policy, and the social status quo' (Bhopal, 1997). In current thinking, 'race' 'is a scientific myth, it persists as a social entity for historical, social and psychological reasons . . .' (Fernando, 1995); 'race' is a 'concept that has largely been discredited in biological science . . .' (Bennett et al., 1995). Currently in the social sciences the term 'race' is placed in quotation marks.

In everyday speech, 'race' almost always refers to differences of skin colour, and is often used in a derogatory manner. In anthropological circles, 'race' has referred to a wide range of genetic characteristics, for example, skin colour, blood group, and hair texture. Reber (1985), however, reminds us that 'race' cannot be defined usefully using only genetic criteria. The whole biological issue is fraught with complexity and contradiction. He concludes that a useful definition of 'race' *must* include a combination of social, political and cultural factors.

For our purposes, the importance of this observation is that the traditional distinction between 'race' (nature) and 'culture' (nurture) cannot be made. Phillips and Rathwell (1986) point out that the study of 'race' has more to do with social relationships, power and domination, than with biological differences.

We do not seek to define 'race'. Instead, we are concerned with *racism*. Fernando (1995) asserts 'Racism is fashioned by racial prejudice and underpinned by economic and social factors'. Thomas (1992) provides a powerful account of the insidious and harmful effect of racism in psychotherapy. He describes how racism even in its covert forms has a countertherapeutic effect on the relationship. Dominelli (1988: 6) points out, '. . . racism is about the construction of social relationships on the basis of an assumed inferiority of non Anglo-Saxon ethnic minority groups and flowing from this, their exploitation and oppression'. We find this a useful definition. But we also note that certain physical characteristics, often described as 'race', result in one person suffering discrimination from another who is in a position of power. These characteristics refer to those aspects of an individual's appearance that distinguish him or her from the dominant culture, which for most of our readers will mean white Anglo-Saxon culture.

WHAT IS TRANSCULTURAL COUNSELLING?

We have chosen the term 'trans' as opposed to 'cross' or 'inter' cultural counselling because we want to emphasise the *active* and *reciprocal* process that is involved. Counsellors in this setting are responsible for working across, through or beyond their cultural differences. Eleftheriadou (1994) emphasises this and states that 'cross' and 'inter' cultural imply that we 'use our own reference system to understand the client's experience rather than going beyond our own worldview'. Clients from other cultures have already had to overcome many barriers in everyday life, and may find the counselling environment a further challenge. Transcultural counselling means that the counsellors accept there is another worldview and try to meet their clients more than halfway.

Leininger (1985) has referred to 'transcultural caring' as using cultural knowledge and skills creatively to help people live and survive satisfactorily in a 'diverse and changing world'. Leininger's emphasis on *intentional* and *positive* processes in the therapeutic relationship is very useful for our model of transcultural counselling. In addition, we stress that transcultural work offers a perspective on counselling rather than a particular school of thought. Our approach to transcultural counselling includes the following components:

- counsellors' sensitivity to cultural variations and the cultural bias of their own approach;
- counsellors' grasp of cultural knowledge of their clients;
- counsellors' ability and commitment to develop an approach to counselling that reflects the cultural needs of their clients;
- counsellors' ability to face increased complexity in working across cultures. This does not mean that such work entails more problems. On the contrary, a properly developed transcultural approach will enrich the skills of all counsellors.

In addition, there are three significant areas in any counselling relationship that begin to take on an added meaning and importance in a transcultural relationship. First, all counselling deals with the establishment of *boundaries*. Both counsellors and clients need to delineate the nature of their relationship and the tasks at hand. The two parties bring expectations and beliefs to counselling which will need to be made explicit and negotiated. For example, clients might come expecting the counsellor to provide them with immediate solutions to their problems. Counsellors, too, might be tempted to prescribe answers without giving clients the opportunity to work through them.

In a transcultural setting, there will be other limits set by the different beliefs about the nature and purpose of problem solving. Boundaries will also need to be drawn regarding the relative *power* of counsellors, as well as the role of clients' other support systems, such as their families and friends. Both parties recognise and agree the limits within which the counselling relationship will function.

6

Secondly, *transference* and *countertransference* have a particular effect in the transcultural setting. The transference of feelings outside the relationship, especially about parents by clients on to their counsellors, is another process that plays a vital part in transcultural counselling. Kareem (1992) observes that both counsellor and client '. . . throughout their lives, carry inner feelings about others and these feelings become accentuated in the therapeutic situation'. This may have a positive, but more often a negative impact on the counselling relationship. Our own view is that transcultural counsellors will actively work to deal with these powerful emotions in ways that we shall demonstrate in the following chapters.

Similarly, countertransference, that is the feelings that are elicited in the counsellor by the client, needs to be recognised and used constructively. The previous experiences and feelings of clients and counsellors will inevitably come to bear on any current counselling and will mould its progress. In a transcultural setting, counsellors will need to see countertransference in terms of the cultural beliefs, prejudices, and racism that is theirs. These additional emotional components are not only active in the counselling relationship, but will affect the clients' attitudes and feelings in all other relationships. Eleftheriadou (1994) concludes that despite substantial personal training, counsellors are not objective and still experience strong emotions towards their clients.

Thirdly, anyone who seeks counselling is in *transition*, that is, moving from one state of being to another. Counselling tasks involve the process of change as a means of achieving personal growth. We often talk about our lives as a journey with stages and pathways. Counselling enables clients to choose the most appropriate pathway through a satisfactory transition. Gilbert and Shmukler (1996) describe the therapeutic environment as a 'transitional space' where clients can try out new ways of expressing themselves in a safe space.

Clients in a transcultural setting must make transitions in a number of different ways. Not only are they dealing with the changes that face us all in personal growth, but they may in addition have to deal with an alienating and often hostile environment. Clients who have suffered these changes and losses have had to develop coping skills (Furnham and Bochner, 1986). These skills can be used by a sensitive counsellor to help clients achieve personal change in counselling.

Finally, transcultural counsellors will be able to examine their own cultural assumptions and face the fears they themselves might have of being separated and alienated. Once counsellors can do this, they become more effective. The term 'transcultural' emphasises the *common* experiences and tasks facing clients and counsellors, who are aware that their values, assumptions and practices are not absolute.

TRANSCULTURAL STUDIES

Transcultural studies have their roots in anthropology and psychiatry, an uneasy alliance which in the twentieth century has centred on the 'validity of applying anthropological modes of thought to the problems posed by the occurrence of mental deviance and emotional suffering in all cultures' (Krause, 1989). Krause (1998) poses the fundamental question about whether modern anthropology, which 'set out to understand others on their own terms' can ever be integrated within psychotherapeutic theories which are universal, disregarding individual difference. In the early 'eighties Littlewood and Lipsedge wrote an influential book that combined theoretical perspectives of psychiatry and social anthropology to describe the mental ill health of minority ethnic groups. They examined the higher incidence of stress and associated mental illness in certain UK cultures. They have offered a very valuable explanation that has implications for all counsellors of a majority culture dealing with minority ethnic clients. They argue that the dominant culture actively alienates people who do not belong to it and produces its own 'aliens'. The 'alienists', as the majority are called, also have no adequate frame of reference for judging the standards of individuals from other cultures. Because of this, they are more likely to describe behaviour that they do not understand as deviant and therefore sick.

Littlewood and Lipsedge (1982; 1997) also refer to the work that demonstrated that Norwegian immigrants were more likely to become mentally ill than the rest of the population. There were, of course, many problems with these early studies; in particular, the failure of the researchers to match the Norwegians with the majority culture for age and sex. Nevertheless it became clear after these corrections had been made that certain groups of immigrants in certain countries were more likely to be treated for psychiatric disorders than non-immigrants. Was it that vulnerable people were more likely than others to emigrate (the selection hypothesis)? Or were the processes of emigration, immigration and settlement themselves damaging and likely to cause mental illness (the stress hypothesis)? The answer was never satisfactorily provided because controlled studies were not carried out.

A further development of the stress hypothesis has been proposed by black mental health researchers, who have argued that racism and ignorance of other cultures can directly and exclusively contribute to mental illness (Burke, 1986). Burke argues that racism maintains social and economic deprivation, limited access to care, and subordination and social control by the majority culture. In this way, other cultures, particularly black ones, are made more vulnerable to physical and psychological ailments, and enter a further cycle of disadvantage. What is being criticised here is not just mental health professionals, or their approach, nor the inadequate services, but an entire political and social system whose laws and practices enable personal and institutional racism to flourish.

Research on immigrants in this field has been of limited value, and has probably contributed much to racism within medical circles; the problems of immigrants were seen as exotic and belonging to them alone. Murphy (1986) has reminded us that racist explanations about large groups of Europeans being 'of poor stock' or 'degenerate' have been made in much the same way as later theorists referred to black people.

In the UK, the popularity of medical genetics and the abuse of Darwinism created increasingly racial and racist accounts of why certain groups of people were more degenerate or tainted than others. Very little was known or researched on what was happening to large groups of individuals who needed or were seeking help in the context of alienation and disadvantage.

Despite a century of research on migration and its consequences, cultural awareness in the helping professions has only developed in the past thirty years. In the USA, the civil rights movement and martyrdom of Martin Luther King had a significant impact on this. Not only was there political change in the status of black people, but also a change in the practice of mental health workers.

In the 1960s, the term 'culture shock' was coined by an anthropologist to describe certain processes experienced by 'cultural travellers' (Furnham and Bochner, 1986). These included: psychological strain, a sense of loss, rejection, confusion, surprise, anxiety and feelings of impotence. Our view of this syndrome is that although it highlights some internal processes for the cultural traveller, it does not take into account the external reality of xenophobia and prejudice.

Triseliotis (1986) reminded us that no emphasis whatsoever has been placed on the *skills* and *strengths* that people from minority ethnic groups have developed out of their adverse experiences. The legacy of this curious omission is that transcultural counsellors have only recently acquired a literature to refer to that is positive, rather than problem bound (Sue and Sue, 1990; Kareem and Littlewood, 1992; Lago and Thompson, 1996).

Conventionally, mental health studies that have looked at differences in disorders between different ethnic groups have been steeped in racist constructs. Fernando (1995) has examined the background to mental health services worldwide, and has concluded, 'Today, the *universalist* psychiatric doctrine, that Western psychiatric concepts – illness-models and treatment needs – have a global relevance, subsumes within it a distinct *racist* judgement of cultures and peoples – often only partially concealed' (1995: 27, our italics). Many studies in the past three decades have addressed the overrepresentation of black people with schizophrenia. Nazroo (1997) observes, 'African Caribbeans are reported to be at least three times more likely than whites to be admitted to hospital with a first diagnosis of schizophrenia'. The literature is extensive, and readers are recommended to original sources such as: McGovern and Cope, 1987; Harrison et al., 1988; Littlewood and Lipsedge, 1988; Cochrane and Bal, 1989. King et al. (1994) take a wider perspective by considering the personal and social pressures of their subjects. In a major prospective study of first onset psychosis of all ethnic groups, they reported a raised level of schizophrenia in *all* groups, and argued that they experienced a higher level of stress which included, 'the effects of migration, discrimination, racism, and cultural change'. Modood et al. (1997) identified socio-economic factors which led to greater distress but Virdee (1997) refers specifically to the effects of harassment on minority ethnic communities. Sashidharan (1993) and Sashidharan and Francis (1993) summarise the serious methodological flaws with studies of the higher rates of psychosis in African-Caribbean people. These include the mistaken premise that higher hospital admission rates are the result of individual pathology, the different meaning attached to a diagnosis of schizophrenia in black and white patients, the bias in case selection which does not control for sociodemographic factors, and the ideology of the researchers in this field.

We have described the contribution of psychiatry so far, because historically, it has emphasised the diagnosis and description of mental disorder in black people, and pathologised them. There has been far less work on psychotherapy and counselling for the problems of 'identity, adjustment, achievement, self-actualisation, personal loss, conflict and resistance' (Littlewood, 1992). In the absence of any systematic, long-term outcome studies of talking therapies for black people, there has been much anecdote, polemic, and political debate.

Psychological studies have fluctuated between on the one hand those which ignore ethnic differences altogether – the 'color blind approach' (Thomas and Sillen, 1972), and on the other hand those which focus on race and differences, particularly intelligence. As late as 1990, the British Psychological Society published in its house journal, *The Psychologist*, an extraordinary 'scientific' debate about I.Q. differences between races, which despite widespread criticism, still gave psychology a very bad press (Rushton, 1990).

Fortunately, there has been a response to this within clinical psychology. There has been a small but vocal group of both black and white professionals who have presented and published work about mental health *needs* and models of service delivery for minority ethnic communities. Good examples of these in the UK include Miller and Thomas, 1994, MacCarthy and Craissati, 1989; Patel (1992), Mahtani and Huq (1993), d'Ardenne (1996), Mullick and Baker (1998), Fatimilehin and Coleman (1998), Newland (1998) and Nadirshaw (1998) have each made contributions about specific minority ethnic communities. Each has identified the psychological needs in their area and how to address them using transcultural models. The agenda has been in part driven by communities themselves who have become more vociferous about unmet need, and counselling, social work, clinical and counselling psychology and psychiatry campaigning groups who have lobbied their own professional bodies. However, there have been no systematic, long-term studies of transcultural counselling in the UK. This state of affairs reflects a wider lack of evaluation of talking therapies, despite their current popularity. In 1996, the British Department of Health published a review of the psychotherapy literature (Roth and Fonagy, 1996). This book highlighted discrepancies between the effectiveness of different models, and different health care groups. Their literature revealed nothing about transcultural work or the impact of racism on mental well-being. Significantly their conclusions provided no research directions for diverse communities nor for cultural and transcultural factors in psychotherapy outcome.

Transcultural counselling practice has developed substantially in the last decade, despite the lack of systematic studies. Pedersen et al. (1996) have offered various reasons for this failure. These include cultural barriers between disciplines connected with research in this field, the complexity of the issues resulting in marginalisation, the traditional emphasis of research on abnormal behaviour that is *independent* of cultural considerations, and the failure to relate any present findings to service delivery.

We propose a *resources and skills-based approach* rather than a problem-orientated one. In the USA, psychologists and counsellors (Pedersen et al., 1996; Sue and Sue, 1990) have developed a body of clinical practice for diverse communities. Emphasis has been placed on pragmatic approaches as well as detailed work on monocultural client populations. As a consequence, there is now an established global literature in the field of transcultural mental health work, including learned journals. In the UK, professional bodies such as the Royal College of Psychiatrists, the British Psychological Society, the British Association for Counselling, and the Central Council for the Education and Training of Social Workers have all begun to develop training programmes which have dealt in their own ways with transcultural work.

Future work has to be done on an interdisciplinary basis. Emphasis on the counselling process across cultures, rather than abnormal behaviour in minority ethnic groups, will provide a more appropriate means of developing culturally sensitive counsellors.

TERMINOLOGY

Terminology in the fields of culture and 'race' is both confusing and controversial. Workers from different professional and personal backgrounds use terms such as 'black' and 'ethnic' for different purposes. We have already offered a working definition of 'culture' and 'race' and have used the term 'minority ethnic group'. Although we work in areas of London where specific ethnic groups are numerically in the *majority*, they are still the *minority* from a social, political and economic standpoint.

The word 'ethnic' is used when we are referring to cultural characteristics of a group of people. Our use of the term 'black' is meant to refer to anyone who could experience racism. Some people from minority ethnic groups do not consider themselves to be black, but many others we know, for example Irish and Turkish people, do call themselves black. We use the two terms 'ethnic' and 'black' interchangeably, in the *political* rather than the biological sense. We prefer not to use the term 'immigrant' because of its association with racism. In the UK, what was previously a neutral term has become linked only to black people in a discriminatory manner. 'Immigrant' has also been used inaccurately to describe British-born black people, and is a term tainted with prejudice.

Fernando (1991) has a clear account of the differences between the terms 'race', 'culture' and 'ethnicity', and Figure 1.1 provides a useful framework to describe the interrelationships between these terms in the context of a racist society.

	Characterised by	Determined by	Perceived as
Race	Physical appearance	Genetic ancestry	Permanent (genetic/biological)
Culture	Behaviour Attitudes	Upbringing Choice	Changeable (assimilation, acculturation)
Ethnicity	Sense of belonging Group identity	Social pressure Psychological need	Partially changeable

FIGURE 1.1 *Race, culture and ethnicity*
Source: Fernando, 1991. Reproduced by kind permission of Macmillan Mind Publications

He concludes that ethnicity is a safer term to use than race, and that it 'has both racial and cultural connotations, but its main characteristic is that it implies a sense of belonging'. However, language is never static; transcultural counsellors remain alert to nuances in meaning, and to how connotations of specific terms change.

THE ROLE OF COMMUNITY GROUPS

While the statutory services have been unable or unwilling to provide multicultural or transcultural facilities, different communities themselves have had to develop their own resources to meet these needs. The British Association for Counselling (Wallbank, 1997) reminds us that many people's first experience of counselling is likely to be with the voluntary sector, who have a wealth of groups devoted to personal need. The National Council for Voluntary Organisations (NCVO) lists over 2,000 entries, itself only a proportion of the total available. These community groups provide a range of services including information, welfare rights, educational programmes, personal and family support. Since the 1950s, with the advent of Carl Rogers' client-centred counselling, many community groups have developed listening as well as advisory roles. Black and minority ethnic organisations recognised the stress and needs of their own communities and counselling. There is evidence in the UK (Ward, 1986) that many of these organisations were established to meet housing or employment needs of a particular ethnic group. Nevertheless, they have had to adopt a counselling or psychotherapeutic role in the light of neglect elsewhere.

Some professional therapists and counsellors have taken a more radical step in their attempts to offer counselling across cultures and work within these voluntary services and the particular ethnic groups they serve. These organisations provide a practical framework for transcultural counselling in action because:

- The statutory services, by their very nature, embody the cultural values, beliefs and prejudices of the majority culture. They have furthest to travel, culturally speaking, to meet the service needs of any client from another culture.
- Community groups are more accessible to other cultures, and lend themselves more easily to locally based programmes, where caring professionals themselves come from the same culture as their clients. A good example of this is the Nile Project in Hackney, East London.
- Community groups provide the most direct vehicle for the expressed needs and wishes of other cultures (Ahmad, 1993; Ward, 1986).
- Self-help community groups also offer the only means of help when existing services show no willingness or commitment to a multicultural approach. NAFSIYAT, an intercultural therapy centre in North London, has pioneered practice, training and research in this area.
- Voluntary programmes are more visible, accessible and sensitive to their users than the statutory services.

Critics of self-help community services have pointed out the risks of their becoming a 'ghetto', where clients have little access to professional input. These critics (e.g. Ahmad, 1993) argue that minority ethnic communities will always receive a second-class service if the voluntary agencies that help them are not properly funded and in collaboration with statutory services. This argument, however, begs the question about why these agencies were established in the first place. Some counsellors have gone out and joined the community agencies to learn about and contribute to transcultural work. Their professional work has done much to improve voluntary services. Liaison has given way to partnership and the joint formation of projects (Lago and Thompson, 1996). These partners are in a unique position to persuade public services to adopt greater responsibility for all communities. Ahmad (1993) observes '. . . one positive consequence of initiatives in community health and in social services is the radicalization of black community activists and a proportion of the black health service workforce'. Consequently, institutional racism is being challenged *from within*.

Fundamental Assumptions

In introducing transcultural counselling, we have made some fundamental assumptions that we would like to share with you. We do not consider our stance on culture to be neutral, as we have been struck by the ethnocentricity of many counsellors. Instead, we have adopted an ethical position about it, which provides us with an underlying framework for practice.

The first of our assumptions is that all cultural groups have *an equal right to benefit from counselling* in our society. This means that where there are groups with specific cultural needs, that appropriate counselling services must be provided.

Secondly, we assume that at present, the *majority culture is hostile* to people from other cultures, at a number of different levels. In counselling, this racism manifests itself in a number of ways, such as counsellors blaming their clients' cultures for their problems, being ignorant of and patronising towards clients, adopting a negative attitude towards black clients' problems, and referring to 'experts' rather than developing their own skills.

Thirdly, in order for all members of society to have equal access to counselling, majority counsellors will need to acknowledge their own *ethnocentricity*. Once counsellors embark on this process, they have the beginnings of a multicultural model of practice. Counsellors at present remain 'culturally encapsulated' when they are unable to see issues from the perspective of another culture.

Our fourth assumption is that culture interacts with other socio-economic factors which affect counselling outcome. These include *gender, class, sexual orientation, and disability*. We have tried to take some of these factors into account, by selecting our case examples from both sexes, and from differing social backgrounds. Inevitably, we have been unable to cover all of these factors despite their significance.

Fifthly, we have tackled both *culture and 'race'* in this book. In our experience, culture is used as a less contentious term when issues of racism are discussed. We have attempted throughout the book to demonstrate the significance of both.

This is a book for counsellors from all cultures. Our approach is essentially *practice-based*. It is also general in the sense that we do not prescribe rules for specific cultures. We assume that counsellors will become culturally sensitive, and that once they become aware, they will go on to investigate particular cultures. From that position, counsellors will provide a more effective transcultural service for their clients.

In the next chapter we shall introduce four clients who will remain with us throughout their counselling relationships. Our choice was determined by the fact that our clients' cultural backgrounds can be clearly distinguished from the mainstream white culture, and pose clear transcultural issues for their counsellors. It so happens that three of these clients migrated to the UK, despite the fact that many black and minority ethnic people are British-born. Our choice is deficient in this respect.

In Chapter 2, we shall use these cases to examine the cultural knowledge of the client. Chapter 3 will then look at cultural knowledge from the counsellor's point of view, and how all cultural knowledge affects the counselling relationship. In Chapter 4 we shall describe the cultural issues involved in getting started in counselling. Chapter 5 is concerned with how counsellors need to find a common language with their clients, both literally and therapeutically. Chapter 6 deals with the established transcultural relationship, and Chapter 7 is about the goals and changes that occur within this relationship. Our last chapter focuses on the end of counselling, and includes practical skills for the completion and termination of counselling.

2

CLIENTS

Overview

In this chapter, we introduce four clients who will stay with us for the rest of the book as they engage in transcultural counselling. We shall then consider issues about clients that need to be identified and understood before counselling even begins, but which will have increasing significance once the relationship has been established. We shall use our four cases to demonstrate these issues. Finally, groups of transcultural clients with additional needs will be considered, together with the implications for counselling in action.

We shall begin by describing the background of four of our clients and the way in which they came to be seen by us in a transcultural setting. Some of their details have been changed to protect their identity, but they remain in essence four people whom we saw outside our own cultures. For the sake of clarity, we present our clients with some details that we subsequently learnt in counselling. Although it may appear that we have made inferences about our clients before seeing them, this is not, in fact, the case.

Figure 2.1 represents our four clients and their counsellors, as well as the relative 'cultural distance' (Furnham and Bochner, 1986) between them. By cultural distance we mean the disparity between two cultures in terms of such issues as food, clothes, shared history, race, climate, religion and family structure (see also Lago and Thompson, 1989).

black counsellor	culturally close	Rahima	black client
	culturally distant	Fred	white client
white counsellor	culturally close	Mathilde	white client
	culturally distant	Clifford	black client

FIGURE 2.1 *Relative cultural distance between counsellors and clients*

We ourselves are two culturally different counsellors; one of us has an Indian background; the other has a white English background. We therefore chose a client each (Rahima and Mathilde) who are our 'culturally close' clients, and a client each (Fred and Clifford) who are our 'culturally distant' clients. In this way we have covered four possible permutations for working across cultures. They raise many of the practical concerns in transcultural counselling, though there are, of course, other possible variables, for example, class and religion.

It has been our experience that counsellors working across cultures flounder when they fail to take into consideration a wide range of *knowledge* that is culturally significant to their clients. Counsellors have no direct control over their clients' cultural experience, but they can anticipate and provide the space for their clients to express themselves in counselling. Culture permeates and affects all aspects of human experience and behaviour. Long before counselling is sought, clients have assets and options that have been shaped by their own cultural contacts. To make transcultural counselling practice-based, we have separated out the components of cultural knowledge into:

- experiences and information
- personal and institutional resources
- attitudes and expectations
- skills
- status
- choices.

We have already referred to the complex and interactional nature of cultural knowledge. In practice, these categories overlap. For example, a client of Vietnamese origin chooses to go to English-language classes, a local institutional resource. She obtains information and experiences of English people, as well as improving her language skills. This in turn affects her attitude and expectations about English culture, and her future status in it.

CASE SUMMARIES

Rahima is a sixty-eight-year-old woman, born and raised in that part of Bengal which is now called Bangladesh. She was well educated and did not pursue a career because she was happily married with two sons and two daughters. At the time of Indian partition in 1947, there were two big changes in her life. First, her husband died suddenly of a heart attack. Then, to compound matters, riots broke out around her home, and made her feel that her children, aged from two to seven years, were at risk. She therefore decided that the future of her family would be better secured if she joined her brother in London.

When Rahima arrived in the UK, she put all her energy into settling her children, and adjusting to a very different lifestyle. She learned to cope with culture shock, and the isolation from the friends and relatives she had left behind. Once the children were all at school, Rahima decided to resume her studies and to train as a lawyer. She qualified and practised successfully for nearly twenty-seven years. Rahima spent all her income on her family and was able to send her older son, Farooq, to boarding school. All her children studied at university and subsequently left her to lead independent lives. Three of them are now married with children of their own.

Rahima has in particular a very turbulent relationship with Farooq. He is the only child to remember her husband, and their life in Bengal. At the time of his father's death, he was thrust into the role of comforting his mother and shouldering responsibility for his brothers and sisters. Over the years he has been more enmeshed with Rahima's life than the other children, and has been in continuous conflict with her.

Shortly before Rahima retired, her brother died. She responded to this second bereavement by spending more time with her children and grandchildren. She lived with them and encountered difficulties with all of them. Rahima has become increasingly weepy and argumentative, and has had a serious row with Farooq. He is very concerned about her, and suggests that she sees a counsellor. She goes to a community centre where an Indian counsellor takes her case on as a client.

Fred was born fifty years ago in the East End of London. He left school at fourteen and spent most of his working life on the docks. He got married at twenty-four to Anne and brought up two sons in a small, two-bedroomed flat. He had several drinking companions, and enjoyed dog racing and playing darts with them.

Three years ago he sustained a back injury which changed his life considerably; he lost his job, and turned to sporadic short-haul lorry driving. As a consequence of these changes, he has become more withdrawn, fearful of crowds, and argumentative with Anne.

Fred has never been close to his children, and has always seen them as coming between him and his wife. His two adult sons live occasionally with him and their visits provoke arguments in his marriage. These arguments concern Anne's abandoning him each day for her job. He complains of increasing difficulty in leaving the flat. His wife works in a well-paid white-collar job with a bank, and enjoys a comfortable and gregarious life away from the home. For his part, Fred spends much of his day isolated and resentful in the home, smoking cigarettes and watching television. Anne eventually refers the problem to their family doctor for help, who recommends a counsellor.

Clifford is a fifty-eight-year-old Nigerian-born car worker who has lived for twenty years in the UK with his wife and son. He suffered for many years with high blood pressure. Two years ago he had a stroke. During his rehabilitation he discovered he had become impotent and informed the staff at the hospital. The doctors were sympathetic, and reassured him that this problem was common and would correct itself without any intervention. Instead, greater emphasis was placed upon his acquisition of fluent speech and rehabilitation for work.

After two years he has made less progress than was expected: his speech remains slurred and he has a pronounced limp. He remains out of work and alone for much of the time at home while his wife goes out cleaning. His son returned to Nigeria to get married and apart from a few relatives in London, Clifford sees virtually nobody. He has once again requested help with his sexual problem, which has not eased with the passage of time. The staff see Clifford as a 'difficult' and 'unco-operative' patient, as his sexual anxieties appear to take precedence over his rehabilitation.

They are also concerned about his isolation, and decide to refer to him a counsellor.

Mathilde is a twenty-eight-year-old Frenchwoman, who used to work as a computer programmer in Aix-en-Provence. She comes from a large rural family, and did well in her schooling and employment. While on a training programme with her company she met her husband, John, who is English. They married soon after and lived both in France and the UK without discussing where they would reside in the future. John's work took him increasingly back to the UK over the following year. At that time Mathilde accidentally became pregnant.

She went into premature labour while on a visit to England, and was obliged to give birth to her first child in London. She had planned to have the baby in France, and was distressed and saddened not to have been able to do so. During her confinement, Mathilde experienced an episode of post-natal depression. She became increasingly weepy and unable to care for herself or her baby. Her husband was concerned and urged her to see a local doctor who treated her with drugs but who also recognised that she needed support. Mathilde speaks some English and spent her time with her doctor asking about maternity benefits and after-care. After several consultations, the doctor realised that Mathilde was struggling with more personal issues, and that she required counselling. Mathilde's doctor knew that she would prefer to speak French, and referred her to an English counsellor with knowledge of French culture and language.

EXPERIENCES AND INFORMATION

In any counselling, the client's previous experiences and knowledge about the counsellor's culture can be used as a framework for change. A counsellor working *across* cultures needs to ascertain which of the client's cultural experiences and knowledge will be of use in counselling. The counsellor will need sensitivity in raising such themes as:

- The extent of the client's knowledge of the counsellor's culture.
- The way in which the client attains this knowledge, for example,
    by living in it
    by being educated in it

through personal relationships
through travel
through books, television and cinema.

- The extent to which the client's knowledge of the counsellor's culture makes counselling easier or more difficult for the client. For example, does this knowledge provide the client with the means of recognising the counsellor's verbal and non-verbal cues?
- Where the client has little shared cultural experience with the counsellor, the extent to which this proves to be a barrier in counselling. For example, the client may be unable to acknowledge, understand or accept the counsellor's culture. Further, the client may be worried about the counsellor's *ability* to work across cultures.

Let's now look at practice, and consider these criteria of cultural knowledge as they would emerge in pre-counselling assessment.

Clifford has spent many years in the UK and is a British citizen. He speaks English and Yoruba and is more fluent in the former. He was educated in Lagos in a church school where most of the syllabus was the same as for English schools of that period. While he was living in Nigeria, most of Clifford's knowledge about English culture came indirectly. He acquired it either from cousins who were already working in the UK, or from the English teachers at his school, or from the many books and films he had seen at that time depicting life in England.

Clifford emigrated to the UK in 1960 at the age of thirty with his wife and son. He worked for most of that time in the car industry as a skilled operator, doing mainly shift-work, and continuing to support several members of his family in Nigeria. He refers to Nigeria as 'home' but now has more Nigerian friends in the UK than in Nigeria. He has returned there only twice, and one of these visits was briefly for a relative's funeral.

Clifford thinks of himself as more Nigerian than English. However, he has adapted to English lifestyle by eating some English food and wearing a suit. He has had experiences of racism from individuals at work, but his friends and family have been supportive and positive enough to help him to cope with it.

Clifford reports that the rehabilitation staff were unable to understand him and the difficulties he had in facing his programme. He in no way construes this as racism.

He has extensive knowledge and experience of the counsellor's culture, some of it acquired vicariously. Although he does not express them, he might have grounds for doubting the ability of a white, English counsellor and her understanding of his culture in counselling. He has had little contact with white professional people, and even less with women. His counsellor will need to take into account these doubts and fears; our next chapter will deal with these in detail.

PERSONAL AND INSTITUTIONAL RESOURCES

Like knowledge and skills, the client's personal and institutional resources can be used positively and creatively by counsellors. Although it is true that many ethnic groups suffer economic hardship, deprivation and racism, transcultural counselling cannot remedy these directly. What it can do is work with clients' assets and help clients use these to the full to achieve personal change. It still occurs that culturally encapsulated counsellors regard some of these resources as 'problems', for example, a close-knit family, a devout religious belief, or political loyalty.

We have included in our list a range of resources that starts with the client as an individual and progresses to partners, families, neighbours, communities, institutions and society at large. Some of these resources are formal and statutory, for example, marriage and education; others are informal, for example, community clubs and friends. The counsellor can identify the client's resources by consideration of such issues as:

Family Resources

- Whether or not the client has a same-culture spouse or partner.
- Whether or not that partner is seen by the client as a resource.
- Those members of the client's family who live at home.
- Those members of the client's family who live in the neighbourhood/district/country.
- The kind of contact the client has with family members, for example, personal, telephone or letter? How often and for how long are they seen?
- The family members that the client sees as significant.
- The client's perception of the family as a resource.

Social Networks

- Whether or not people from the same culture as the client live nearby.
- The client's access to groups from this culture that are active in the

community, for example, offering information, support, liaison, facilitating cultural values.
- The client's friends who are from the same or a different culture.

Religious Resources

- Whether or not the client has and/or practises a religion.
- The facilities available for worship.
- The type of help, including counselling, available from the religious community.

Health Care

- Whether or not the client who has problems, including emotional ones, uses health professionals who are themselves culturally sensitive.
- The client's use of 'traditional' healers from the same culture as an alternative treatment resource.
- Whether or not the client has access to advocacy and interpreting services.

Political Beliefs

- The political circumstances, if any, surrounding the client's status prior to counselling, for example, refugee status.
- Those political beliefs and loyalties which sustain the client in another culture.
- The client's use of political groups as a resource.
- Whether the political climate in which the client presently lives is a tolerant one.

Education

- Those culturally sensitive resources available to the client still in formal education, for example, multicultural anti-racist class activities.
- The impact of the client's educational achievement on cultural or racial prejudice.

Employment

- The client's current employment status, and whether there are members of the same cultural group in the work setting.

- The cultural sensitivity of the client's employer.
- Whether the unemployed client can meet other members of the same community through local activities and centres.

Rahima comes to counselling and is carefully assessed for her resources. In spite of the conflict she has with them, her children are her biggest asset. She comes to counselling viewing her children as a problem, but simply through the questions posed by the counsellor, comes to see them as a cultural resource. She has lived with all of them, and their children, and derives great emotional support from them.

She does have occasional contacts with a local Asian women's association, and has some friends from this. Her brother had been her only relative in the UK, and the one who provided emotional support to Rahima and all her family. After his death and Rahima's retirement, there was a void, leading to greater tension between Rahima and her children.

Her home is in a mainly white area, and she has few Asian neighbours. At the first session she says she prefers the company of people with Indian cultural heritage, especially professionals. She still keeps in touch with one or two Indian lawyers in her old law firm, but most of her acquaintances are white English, and she describes them as being part of a polite and distant culture.

Rahima's educational and professional achievements give her a valuable resource in terms of her role in UK society. Largely through her own endeavours, she has achieved economic self-reliance and security. She has worked and studied in two different cultures, and has herself experience of working in a transcultural setting As a lawyer, she has listening and advocacy skills, themselves a resource which enable her to benefit more fully from counselling.

ATTITUDES AND EXPECTATIONS

Clients come into all counselling carrying expectations and attitudes about the content of counselling sessions, about the process, and about the counselling relationship. The questions that clients bring to transcultural counselling reflect their experiences and relationships across cultures beforehand. They may also include discrepancies between their own cultural beliefs and those of their counsellors. These will include such issues as:

- Whether or not the client perceives the counsellor's culture or race as a cause of the present problem.

- The client's perception of culture or race as a solution to the problem.
- The client's expectation that the counsellor holds similar attitudes to him or herself, and if not, the extent to which this will affect the counselling relationship.
- The client's view of power in relation to the culture of the counsellor.
- Whether or not the client's culture has some bearing on expectations about the outcome of counselling.
- The client's experience of prejudice outside counselling, for example, racism.
- Whether or not the client's prejudices have any bearing on the counselling relationship, for example, if the client is white and the counsellor is black.
- Whether or not the client is able to accept, acknowledge and understand the counsellor's culture.

We have put these questions explicitly: clients do not necessarily pose these directly when they are being assessed, but they can form a large hidden agenda before transcultural counselling begins.

Fred has already dealt with the questions about acceptance and understanding from a person of another culture through his relationship with the Indian doctor who initially referred him to the Indian counsellor. Fred worries much more about being accepted as a working-class man in his neighbourhood where there are many 'yuppies' whom he sees as changing and dominating the quality of his local life. This view is complicated by his perception of his wife as already having higher materialistic expectations and achievements than himself. His attitude towards Asian people in East London is that they are working-class like himself who are also trapped by poverty and who are just as powerless as he is to prevent the changes that he sees occurring around him.

His Indian counsellor is a professional middle-class woman whom he sees as being very powerful and knowledgeable. He so closely identifies her with his Indian doctor that he assumes that the two are relatives (they are not!). From this, he assumes that she will work 'competently', but has, as yet, no definite ideas about working across cultures. Neither does he yet know whether she will acknowledge, accept or understand his East London culture.

The fact that the counsellor is a woman is significant; Fred clearly has difficulties in accepting changes in his power relationship with his wife, and feels threatened by this. He is less than comfortable at exposing this difficulty to a younger woman who is also from another culture, and faces counselling with very mixed feelings.

SKILLS

Nobody comes into counselling without skills. These can be linguistic, social, intellectual, interpersonal or technical. In addition, clients from other cultures have had to acquire these skills cross-culturally (Furnham and Bochner, 1986). They argue that the purpose behind these skills is to enable culturally different people to cope successfully with an alien culture without necessarily surrendering their own culture in the process.

If counsellors are to help their clients cope with living in a new culture, then it will be necessary for them to establish clients' existing skills. In assessing a client from another culture, the counsellor will need to ascertain:

- The client's basic interpersonal skills across cultures. for example,
    assertiveness
    posture and distance
    eye contact
    carrying out ritualised greetings.
- The particular abilities of a client from a collectivist culture, that is, one where individual needs are subordinate to those of the community, for example,
    consultation
    achieving group solutions.
- The particular abilities of a client from an individualistic culture, that is, one where individual needs come before the community, for example,
    personal enterprise and achievement
    individual decision making.
- The client's verbal communication skills, for example,
    method of expressing such feelings as anger, grief or fear
    listening skills.
- The client's ability to speak fluently in the same language as the counsellor.
- Whether or not this shared language is the client's first language.
- Whether or not the client has acquired cultural skills, including learning a new language, as a direct result of being in an alien culture.

In practice, then, *Mathilde* comes to the UK as a skilled, professional woman who has some knowledge about English culture. She has slightly improved her schoolgirl English as a result of wanting to be able to communicate with John. This has not always been successful, and their language of intimate communication remains French. Mathilde thus uses the two languages for different types of communication. Before counselling begins, she is able to recognise that there are some subjects she is able to discuss comfortably in English. But those topics nearer to her emotional problems flow more easily when she is able to express them in her first language.

She comes from a large family in the south of France and her Catholic, Mediterranean background is one where she is accustomed to expressing herself with forceful assertiveness. Her feelings are close to the surface, but one of the first skills she learns in English culture is how to control those feelings and present a more phlegmatic view of herself to her husband's family. She does not believe that she has lost any of her personality in doing this, as she readily reverts to type when she meets someone from her home town, or even when she is on the telephone to France.

She has learnt to live more independently in England and to use personal resources that were previously untapped. She no longer has her family around her and she has therefore learnt to drive a car, has opened her own bank account, and registered for English language courses at evening class. At an emotional level, Mathilde had started to develop new skills for her new life in England until the baby was born. She had made a few English friends and trusts and uses them much more than she would have done in France where she turned to her mother for support and advice. She communicates her ideas with clarity and despite her difficulties, is able to make decisions that will leave her feeling in more control in an alien culture.

STATUS

How do clients see themselves *vis-à-vis* the dominant culture and how do they see the status of the counsellor? If counsellor and client come from the same or similar cultures, the picture may be further complicated by professionalism. In our experience, clients from ethnic groups perceive counsellors of their own culture positively. However, there are occasions when these clients are unhappy about seeing same culture counsellors, whom they may see as having 'sold out' to the establishment. They may also judge their black counsellor as having less power and status than white counsellors. Thus, perceived and actual status are intimately linked and will have a profound effect on the outcome of counselling across cultures. What matters is the client's view of status, and the recognition and acknowledgement of that status by the counsellor, who will then use its meaning in the counselling relationship.

In a transcultural setting, clients will see the specific status and power of their own culture in relationship to their counsellor's by means of:

- their cultural and linguistic fluency in the majority culture
- their educational background
- their socioeconomic status
- their gender
- their own employment
- their view of the professional role of counsellor.

Rahima sees herself in relation to her counsellor as a fellow-Asian who can communicate with her in Hindi and Bengali, as well as English. Once counselling has started, Rahima will be able to explore other aspects of her status, including such themes as:

- Whether or not her background will be better understood by her counsellor.
- Whether or not the counsellor will be empathic to her immediate experiences as an Asian in the UK.
- Whether or not she will be more sympathetic to her needs.
- The relevance of their both being professional women.

However, Rahima's status is different from her counsellor's in a number of ways:

- her age;
- her dress; Rahima wears traditional saris; her counsellor does not;
- her employment status and consequent earning power;
- her religious background;
- her family and marital status.

Rahima is probably in two minds about her status with this counsellor. Though she feels pleased to see an Indian counsellor, Rahima is daunted by her youth and her Western appearance. She will be able to explore her status during the counselling process.

CHOICES

Clients have fewer choices than counsellors – a fact that is only recently being recognised within counselling services. An acknowledgement of this at the start of the counselling process can be an empowering experience which we will explore more fully in Chapter 4.

Minority ethnic and black clients are occasionally offered access to counsellors of their own culture, when they are available or when it is presumed that there are fewer problems than working cross-culturally. When talking about status, we noted that not all black and minority ethnic clients want to see someone from the same background as themselves. What they may be seeking are culturally sensitised counsellors. The counselling process should enable clients to make personal choices, but they are often given little or no choice in the referral process.

With *Mathilde* for example, the birth of her child and the subsequent depression partly determined her choice to use a doctor to begin talking about her problems. She could have chosen to receive her 'medicine' quite passively, but decided when counselling was offered, that more talking was necessary. Thereafter, it was the doctor who helped her to decide where and with whom she spoke. The doctor recognised that although she was treating Mathilde for a post-natal illness, there was a need for psychological help. She was willing to see Mathilde for longer periods herself but knew of a French-speaking counsellor and offered this person as a more appropriate resource to the client. Mathilde's choices were therefore:

- whether or not to opt for counselling;
- whether or not to accept her doctor's choice of counsellor;
- whether to work with a man or a woman;
- whether or not to work in her first language.

It was made clear to Mathilde that another counsellor could be sought if she was unable to establish a working relationship with her doctor's choice.

SPECIFIC CLIENT GROUPS

Counsellors need to give further consideration to certain client groups across cultures who suffer additional discrimination. These include women, the elderly, the young, refugees, disabled people, and sexual minorities, but we recognise that there are more.

WOMEN

Ussher and Nicolson (1992) describe how the gender balance within UK psychology has shifted towards women, and created a growing interest in feminist psychology, and the psychological needs of all women, black and white. The British Psychological Society, after much debate, acceded to the Psychology of Women Section in 1988.

Watson and Williams (1992) observe, 'Indeed, the difficulties faced by black women . . ., by women of poverty . . ., by women with disabilities . . . and by women with major mental health difficulties . . . have still not been substantially addressed.' They point out that racial and sexual inequalities have interactive and cumulative effects, which impact on the higher incidence in black women with a diagnosis of chronic mental illness, the sanctioning of sexual abuse and violence, and the dispossession of their history. Holland (1995) provides an important model which integrates the effects of social and political issues on women's mental health, a process known as 'social action psychotherapy'. She established a project in a multiracial inner city housing estate in London, and was able to provide a service for women deemed 'unsuitable' by traditional psychotherapy services. Clients were empowered both individually and collectively to deal with their personal, social and political problems.

Smith pointed out (1985a) that there were *no* texts on counselling black or minority women, despite the fact that they had as high rates of alcoholism as black men, and as high rates of suicide as white women. She refers to research that shows that counsellors tend to avoid accepting black women as clients because so many of their problems are environmentally caused, and are, it is presumed, not subject to any direct influence by the counselling process. In the context of social casework, Cheetham (1981, 1982) has described some of the principles of good practice; and recommends more research into the counselling needs of black women and consequent service provision. Bhavnani and Haraway (1994) have edited an excellent collection of papers addressing these issues in a feminist context.

Littlewood and Lipsedge (1982) view women as a culturally disadvantaged group, and consider the Marxist viewpoint that they have a similar history of oppression as non-Europeans. Our own thinking is that black women are doubly disadvantaged in Anglo-Saxon society; both their sex and their race become barriers to finding appropriate counselling services. For example, NAFSIYAT (1985), a London-based Intercultural Therapy

Centre, found that black women were under-represented in their referrals, even at this specialist centre.

What, then, is happening to this important group of people? Increasingly, women are turning to each other for information, self-help and support groups in their own communities. Women in these groups then begin to share their experiences and difficulties, as a result of which informal counselling sessions begin. There is evidence (Maternity Services Liaison Scheme, 1984) that self-help, advocacy and liaison may still provide the first, and for some the only, counselling contact for women where there is a considerable degree of isolation. More professional contact is only available to women who have had to overcome some of these first hurdles, either alone or with others.

OLDER ADULTS

Older people frequently have less access to mainstream society. The formal educational and employment settings provided for the young are simply not available to them. Thus they have fewer opportunities to learn about their new culture, should they wish. Old people are neglected, sadly, in many cultures, and there is an attitude within the majority culture that minority communities look after their own. Webb-Johnson (1991) examines this stereotype in the context of the extended family. Many white people believe that Asian elders are cared for by their children and grandchildren. In fact, she quotes Brown (1984) who found that only 16% of Asian families in the UK fitted this description. Webb-Johnson (1991) furthermore considers the intergenerational tensions that may arise within the home, which may add stress to all concerned.

John (1981) quotes a survey of 1,380 Asian families in the West Midlands, UK, where the elderly were still living with their younger relatives in their homes, but where relationships had become very strained. The elderly were no longer the heads of the household, nor financially independent. Some elderly people had hopes of returning to their homeland once they had made enough money. Often, they lost their remaining relatives at home, and became increasingly isolated and neglected in their adopted country. Their counselling tasks are complicated by the unfulfilled expectations that they may have suffered, with the further loss of role and esteem within their own immediate family setting. Alston et al. (1992) have examined loneliness in black elderly people, and found that unmarried black women were more likely than married or widowed counterparts to feel hopeless. Baker (1994) looked at the psychiatric treatment of older African Americans in a biopsychosocial context. They emphasised the importance of including African values of community and family, and historic events that have affected them, as part of improving treatment outcome.

CHILDREN AND YOUNG PEOPLE

Black youngsters experience the racism and cultural disadvantage shared with all age groups in alternative cultures. But in addition to this they also have to cope with all the personal crises of growing up. They have needs in vocational choice, job preparation, dealing with family conflicts and the painful struggles for independence.

All of these tasks have to be placed within the context of conflicting values with the dominant culture, and the sense of powerlessness and anger bred from personal and institutionalised racism. These difficulties may present as a clash between the values of individual young people and their families. Indeed, the family may represent yet another culture with which the youngster cannot identify, and from which escape has to be sought.

Durrant (1986) reminds us that even pre-school children have a racial and cultural awareness and that because most small black children have now been born in the new culture does not mean that they do not have particular needs. She refers to the work of Milner (1983) that showed that children as young as three or four, especially of African-Caribbean origin, significantly undervalued their own group and preferred their white peers. That such young people should undervalue, or in some cases reject, their own identity so early in life has enormous implications for later self-esteem and counselling tasks.

Phoenix (1997) has discussed how 'race' and ethnicity affect early childhood. She urges professionals to deal with these issues explicitly in order to achieve good practice. Tizard and Phoenix (1995) interviewed 58 adolescents of mixed parentage and found a wide variety of racial identities and cultural allegiances, which were in part related to schooling, social class and politicization about 'race'. They consider the implications for interracial adoption and fostering in an area that remains fraught with controversy and heated debate.

REFUGEES

Counselling and mental health services for refugees and asylum seekers remain grossly inadequate in most Western countries. Many statutory services fail to provide basic communication or access for whole communities additionally distressed by political repression, detention, torture and violence, the disappearance of relatives, separation and loss, hardships and exile (Van der Veer, 1992). Richman (1998) observes that the literature on distress in refugees in the West tends to focus on the effects of past events in the country of origin. She highlights a number of factors in the country of exile that have an effect on their mental health, such as separation from the family, isolation from their own community, an inability to speak the new language, loss of socioeconomic status, and an unfriendly host community. In their study of male Iraqi refugees who had been tortured, Gorst-Unsworth and Goldenberg (1998) reported that a lack of social support was a stronger predictor of long-term depression than was the severity of the previous trauma. They suggest that family reunion and support by culturally competent workers are important ways of alleviating distress. These are political as well as professional issues that must be tackled when working with refugee people and emphasise the importance of the services provided in the here and now.

Winter and Young (1998) have quoted Jaranson and Bamford (1987) who have distinguished four different models of service delivery in the US: the psychiatric model, the community mental health model, the primary health care clinic model, and the multiservices or social services model. Winter and Young conclude that the primary health care model is the most integrated, whereas the multiservices model provides a service to a greater number of refugees.

The debate in the literature has centred on the applicability of Western approaches to distress in refugee communities. Summerfield (1998) argues, 'War-affected populations are largely directing their attention not inwards, to "trauma", but outwards, to their devastated social world.' He warns that if these issues are ignored, there is a danger of failure as the Western approach will be seen as irrelevant. Bracken (1998) critiques the application of Post Traumatic Stress Disorder as a universally applicable concept. It is important to examine the cultural context of the refugee client and incorporate this within therapeutic work. Winter and Young (1998) have listed barriers to intervention including cultural beliefs about the origins of mental disorder, the so-called lack of psychological-mindedness of clients, and the unfamiliarity of disclosure outside the family. They review recent work in the field which suggests that when a therapeutic alliance has been established, transcultural counselling with refugees can be effective.

DISABLED PEOPLE

A useful model of physical disability (Oliver, 1990; Swain et al., 1994) is one which emphasises society's disabling environments and attitudes, rather than the impairment of the individual. Many disabled people prefer the term 'disabled people' because it refers to disablement as something that society does to individuals, rather than the personal characteristics of impairment. This is a social rather than a medical model, and one which sits comfortably with a transcultural model, that highlights the strengths of clients rather than pathologising them. Transcultural counsellors who work with disabled people must recognise the cultural, physical and social barriers created by society. A related issue is whether healthcare staff are aware of the increased prevalence of certain conditions, for example sickle cell trait or thalassaemia in minority ethnic populations. Black and minority ethnic people are disadvantaged because they often have less information about statutory services. CVS (1997) suggests a strategy for empowering black disabled people which includes: involvement in the planning stages, outreach work, translated and user-friendly information, use of community networks and provision of training and support to service users. Morris (1991) asserts that there are similar issues that affect those with learning disabilities as those with physical disabilities. Nadirshaw (1997) has pointed out that there are no UK figures on the prevalence of learning disability among black and minority ethnic communities, but that there are local figures that give rise to concern. She cites the literature that shows the higher rates of children and young adults with severe learning disabilities in the Asian community. There are no equivalent data however for African-Caribbean communities. It is worth noting some of the beliefs that she observes in various Asian communities that need to be understood for those counselling families affected by disabilities.

SEXUAL MINORITIES

Gay and lesbian clients from minority ethnic communities, suffer discrimination at a number of levels. They may already have experienced difficulties within their own families, in getting jobs, and being accepted within the gay community. Their health is also more at risk. Wright (1993) describes African American men as being disproportionately affected by HIV. They do not always fit traditional sexual identity categories (i.e. heterosexual, bisexual, and homosexual) and he suggests that a more sensitive health education and intervention be offered to them. Recently there have been more attempts to open up descriptions beyond these categories; for example, 'men who have sex with men'. This is of particular relevance to people whose language does not incorporate a word for 'gay', 'lesbian' or 'homosexual'.

BHAN (Black HIV and AIDS Network) is one UK voluntary organisation that has highlighted the combined effects of racism and living with HIV and AIDS in the UK, and provides practical support for them. Bhatt (1991) criticises the use of Western counselling and its emphasis on individualism. The results can prove disastrous, and can mean the end of family and community support without any alternatives. There remain very few dedicated services for black gay and lesbian people in the UK. They are obliged to use organisations whose main focus is HIV/AIDS rather than their specific psychosexual needs.

IMPLICATIONS FOR PRACTICE

As far back as 1985, NAFSIYAT reminded us of the dangers of making the transcultural problem so much the salient issue, that we forget what clients have in common with the rest of their contemporaries and treat them as exotic or delicate creatures.

Keeping this cautionary note in mind, we have developed the following ideas about good practice, both from working with community organisations, from our own clinical practice, and from the expanding literature (Kareem and Littlewood, 1992; Holland, 1995; Lago and Thompson, 1996). These ideas create a framework within which transcultural counselling becomes more effective, as we shall demonstrate throughout this book.

First, due consideration has to be given to socio-economic issues such as housing, money, and unemployment. Giving credence to the external stressors in the lives of minority ethnic clients establishes counsellors' understanding and trustworthiness, as well as creating a safe therapeutic milieu.

Second, we need to understand more about how minority ethnic clients access talking therapies. For example, working-class Asian people are more likely to select a physical complaint than an emotional one because they believe that that is what their doctor would find more acceptable, (Littlewood and Lipsedge, 1997). Counsellors have to help those referrers increase their awareness of emotional communication.

Third, clients who have emigrated have to adjust their own social and gender roles within their families and community. This is an immensely complex and delicate situation, which encompasses the rules of differing societies, of culture, kinship and religion, all of which are themselves in transition. Counsellors can use their professional networks, their supervisors, and community organisations to struggle with these issues, in a way that informs their transcultural work.

Fourth, we have observed that these recently arrived clients often use their own established community networks, prior to being referred for formal counselling. It is within the safety of a single-culture group that they can share common feelings and stress, as well as skills and information. They may also hear about and understand that there are other kinds of help available. Counsellors and community workers can collaborate on this preparatory task through outreach work within those communities.

In addition, lack of childcare facilities is a major concern for *women*, (Watson and Williams, 1992), particularly in under-resourced minority ethnic associations. In practice, we find it may be necessary to find a childminder during counselling. Failing that, we break with convention, and see a woman in the presence of her small children, and learn to share this distraction with her.

Finally, a note of caution about feminist approaches in counselling across cultures. Washington (1980) reminds us that white feminists have marginalised black women in literature. Watson and Williams (1992) point out that racism has been judged to be secondary to the issue of gender in black women's lives. Furthermore, they argue that white women have to take responsibility for developing alternative models of service delivery that take account of the impact of racism. Counsellors working with a western model are in danger of judging the sexism of another culture only from their own standpoint. All societies are sexist; the way they express it differs. In practice, we have to refrain from judging our women clients as being sexually oppressed. Instead we listen to our clients' cultural norms, and try to work with women and their partners in the dilemmas that we all face. Counselling teaches us to be non-judgemental, but when we hear about abusive relationships, it is hard not to allow our own values to affect the counselling process. There are no easy solutions.

In conclusion, we have looked at the cultural knowledge that our clients bring to counselling across cultures. This is, of course, only one side of the picture. Counsellors too have cultural knowledge, and in the following chapter we shall describe how best this can be used in practice.

3

Counsellors

Overview

Having looked at clients, we shall now consider counsellors and the types of cultural knowledge that are brought to transcultural counselling before meeting the client. Once again, we will consider cultural knowledge in the six categories of experiences and information, personal and institutional resources, attitudes and expectations, skills, status and choices. We shall then use the four cases, introduced in the last chapter, to highlight what cultural knowledge means in practice, and how transcultural counselling is influenced by this knowledge even before it begins.

This chapter is about the counsellor, and the cultural knowledge you need in order to work transculturally. As we pointed out in the last chapter, counsellors often fail to consider clients' cultural knowledge and, by the same token, disregard their own. Like your client, you can recognise and develop this knowledge. Once you have done this, you will be better equipped to work transculturally. You have, however, different responsibilities and knowledge from your clients, and will need to build on those components of cultural knowledge accordingly.

Sue and Sue (1990) have proposed two practical ways in which counsellors can improve their effectiveness in a transcultural setting. The first is when counsellors and clients share the same *world view.* By this they mean that the counsellor understands and accepts the client's cultural/racial heritage, experiences in society and ethnic identification. Sue and Sue

(1990) are not, however, suggesting that counsellors have to hold the same views as their clients. The counsellor is able to use this view with the client to establish goals which are appropriate to the client's culture. A practical example of this is the following instance regarding Rahima.

Rahima has recently had difficulties with all four of her children, and threatened to sever all ties with them. Her counsellor recognises the greater importance of family bonds in her Bengali culture compared to others. She understands Rahima's world view and sees beyond her immediate distress. She will use this knowledge in the counselling process.

The second means of enhancing transcultural effectiveness is when the counsellor uses the same counselling modalities as the client. By this, Sue and Sue (1990) mean that counsellors anticipate working in ways that are consistent with the life experiences and cultural values of the client. In our case, *Clifford's* counsellor considers that a more directive approach in counselling will be more effective and appropriate in Nigerian culture.

As counsellors, we often take for granted our own culturally held views when seeing our clients, and we rarely question them. Even when we face clients' different cultural views, we seldom look at our own values more critically. Lago and Thompson (1996) refer to the 'realm of self-understanding' that gives us insights into the cultural positions of others 'through our empathy and through our imagination'. They suggest that we cannot examine our own cultures without the assistance of 'cultural outsiders'. There are, of course, dangers in all cultural relativism, which we have already discussed in Chapter 1. This chapter will deal with the counsellor's cultural standpoint, and demonstrate how best to gain knowledge across cultures.

COUNSELLOR'S EXPERIENCES AND INFORMATION

Let us consider any experiences and information you may have as counsellors about cultures other than your own and, in particular, any specific information you may have about your client's culture. This kind of knowledge often comes from a curiosity and a desire to make contact with these cultures. This is one type of information; there are of course different levels and types of information. Direct contact through kinship, friendship or travel, is bound to be a very different experience than indirect contact with a culture, for example, through reading, second-hand accounts or the media. But counsellors have individual styles and needs too. You may make friends with neighbours from another culture, or you can read literature that introduces you to a culture. What matters is that you seek information and experience of other cultures in all possible ways that are around you.

Before seeing a client from another culture, you, as counsellors, will therefore need to consider the following issues:

- Your range of intercultural experiences and information outside counselling.
- Whether or not you got this information
    (a) actively, e.g. reading, the internet or travel or
    (b) by circumstances, e.g. being born in a multicultural neighbourhood, being educated in a multicultural school.
- The specific knowledge you have of your client's culture.
- Whether or not you have had personal experiences of cultural prejudice or racism.
- Whether or not your experiences and information will be used in the counselling relationship.

If we look at the case of *Mathilde,* her counsellor did have some intercultural knowledge prior to seeing her client. This included four years working in Belgium, during which two of her children had been born. Belgian culture is French-speaking, with many shared values and beliefs of French culture. It is similar enough for the counsellor to have had a similar experience about having a baby in another culture. The information that the counsellor had obtained about French culture had initially been achieved through visits and holidays to France, and from what she had learnt in school from studying the French language. Here she had also learnt about French history, the importance of family life, politics, philosophy and art, and their lifestyle. These experiences were active and sought after, and disposed the counsellor positively towards French culture and people. The counsellor believes that she will be able to use this cultural information and these experiences constructively in the counselling relationship. She feels able to empathise with a client who has given birth 'on the wrong side of the Channel'. The counsellor intends to use her experience as a credential to counsel her client.

The fact that Mathilde is culturally close to the counsellor does not necessarily make transcultural counselling any easier. The client has given birth against her will in another country; the counsellor has not. The client has a husband of a different culture; the counsellor has not. The client has a strong ambivalence towards her marriage; the counsellor has not. What connects each of them to each other is the experience of giving birth away from home.

The counsellor's ability to work effectively with Mathilde in cultural terms will depend on other cultural knowledge too, for instance her skill at speaking French. In addition, there will also be her resources, her attitudes, her status and her choices.

PERSONAL AND INSTITUTIONAL RESOURCES

Counsellors' resources enable them to develop their cultural experiences and information. In our last chapter, every aspect of the client's life was considered as a resource in transcultural counselling. This began with the individual and progressed out to a wide network of relationships and organisations, both in the local community and in society at large. Counsellors also have many networks both within and beyond counselling which need to be identified.

Not only do you have access to private resources; you are much more likely to be linked to establishment and institutional groups that can be used effectively to help achieve knowledge about other cultures. You do not have to get all your knowledge from books. Consider such issues as:

Family Resources

- Whether or not you or a member of your family are from another culture, and whether this experience helps you in counselling.
- Whether or not you or a member of your family have travelled and worked in another country, and whether this adds to your cultural knowledge.

Social Networks

- If you have friends or neighbours from a culture different to your own, and you are able to draw on their experiences to help your transcultural clients.
- Whether or not there are community facilities for different cultural groups in your neighbourhood.

Religious Resources

* If you have religious beliefs, whether or not you are able to use them to be sensitive and tolerant to other cultural beliefs.

Health Care

* If you have ever had therapy (such as acupuncture, herbalism, yoga), whether or not that has given you insight into another culture.

Political Beliefs

* Whether or not your political beliefs help you in your tolerance and understanding of other cultures, and the world at large.

Education and Training

* Whether or not you currently have access to *multicultural education* or training.

Employment

* Whether or not the organisation in which you work is committed to challenging racism.
* Whether or not your employer provides multicultural facilities such as interpreters, cultural information, advocacy and liaison.

Once you have exhausted these more immediate resources, you can then pursue specialist facilities in the wider community, which include:

* intercultural therapy centres;
* workshops and training;
* race relations organisations;
* community organisations for minority ethnic groups.

We have listed these broader categories of resource and hope that culturally sensitive counsellors can use them both for their own development, as well as their clients'.

In *Fred's* case, the counsellor uses many personal and institutional resources. She knew in advance that her client was a white working-class man, and that he lived in an area of London known for its overt racism and hostility towards Asians. She herself has lived in the UK for many years and has had to cope continuously with hostile attitudes in her personal and occupational environment. In order to understand Fred better, she uses her many white friends and acquaintances to provide her with insights into the prejudices and fears expressed by the majority culture.

She has had supervision and is in contact with several discussion and support groups for black counsellors, who help her make sense of all her transcultural experiences. In the case of Fred, she knows in advance that she will be able to use these groups if the need arises. She also has a network of family and black friends who provide her with the support and understanding to deal with these problems.

Her social and political education enable her to understand racism and make her less judgemental of her clients, whatever their cultural or racial background. However, she is aware that racism is an extremely emotive issue, which will continue to challenge the counselling relationship and the counsellor. The counsellor's formal education has provided her with little chance to explore cultural beliefs and prejudices. Because of this, she has used current training to develop these areas of interest and importance. She is able to use all these resources to approach Fred's problems in a more competent and caring way.

ATTITUDES AND EXPECTATIONS

We have already listed the information and resources that counsellors can call upon when working with clients across cultures. But cultural knowledge of any kind is of little value if counsellors, whether black or white, cannot critically examine their own attitudes and expectations.

Attitudes are difficult to change, and counsellors are no different from others in not wishing to acknowledge their own racism or cultural prejudice. Counsellors rarely display open hostility to their clients, but are capable of showing more subtle forms of racism and cultural prejudice. Black workers (Sue, 1981; Burke, 1986; Fernando, 1995) have had to help counsellors from all cultures to look at their attitudes. These workers have had to deal with their racist clients and the hostility that this creates, with very little recognition or responsibility from white counsellors. As a result of black mental health lobbying, some white workers (e.g. Katz, 1978) have also begun to help white counsellors examine their own racism.

Smith (1985b) has described the 'myth of sameness'. She refers to counsellors who 'bury their heads in the sand' and who protest that the only essential attitude required in counselling is one that contains empathy. She then describes why empathy is a necessary quality for counsellors, but is certainly not sufficient for effective transcultural counselling. All counsellors have historically held attitudes and expectations about their own culture, which are inevitably biased. This bias becomes the foundation of prejudice when counselling a client transculturally. Counsellors should be very careful when insisting that they are non-judgemental with all their clients, regardless of colour or creed. You may be rationalising and avoiding difficult cultural and racial conflicts within yourself.

In practice, counsellors' attitudes and expectations can be as much a 'problem' as those of the client from another culture. Where there are problems, it may be difficult for clients to tackle their counsellor's prejudices and subsequent expectations of outcome. The power difference between them makes this an unlikely scenario. It is therefore up to counsellors to take responsibility for their own cultural and racial biases and to understand, for example, the effect that low expectations may have on your clients' success.

As far back as 1972 Thomas and Sillen presented a continuum of attitudes in which white therapists view their black clients. At one extreme, they proposed that clients bear 'the mark of oppression' where the behaviour of black people is seen as pathological. In this model, black people became the 'handicapped victims of racism'. Even when viewed sympathetically, they became dehumanised by white people, including therapists. At the other end of the spectrum, white liberal therapists could be 'colour blind', that is they could minimise the consequences of racial oppression and treat their black clients as 'a white man in a black skin' (Thomas and Sillen, 1972: 65). This model enables counsellors to locate themselves in relation to their black clients and their problems. In addition, this continuum puts into perspective the attitudes of other helping professionals in their dealings with black clients.

But we suggest that there may be other practical issues for you as a counsellor to consider, such as:

- how your cultural or ethnic background affects your attitude to your client;
- whether or not you see the client's culture or ethnicity as a cause of the present problem;
- whether or not you see the client's culture as part of the solution to the present problem;

- whether or not you can accept, acknowledge and understand your client's culture;
- whether or not your expectations about the client's culture affect the counselling outcome;
- whether or not your cultural prejudice has a bearing on the counselling relationship;
- whether or not any cultural prejudice or racism experienced by you affects the counselling relationship;
- whether or not your expectations of the Western model affect the counselling relationship and outcome.

Let us look at one of our practical examples. *Clifford's* difficulties were seen as being of 'cultural' origin by the various therapists who were responsible for his rehabilitation programme after his stroke – what Thomas and Sillen (1972) would call his 'mark of oppression'. He was referred because he was not progressing in his therapy and had become increasingly frustrated with the clinical staff. They could not understand the cause of his frustration and began to describe him as a 'problem' patient, for whom there was little they could do. On the other hand, the doctors who saw him were 'colour blind', and made no reference to his ethnicity, nor did they assess the importance of his cultural values.

Both these therapeutic endeavours, different as they appear to be, had the same effect of dehumanising Clifford. In counselling Clifford, the counsellor takes into account the impact of all these experiences on the way he expresses himself.

But the counsellor has to look at herself too. Her attitude may be that she is not prejudiced and that counselling is a helping process for people whatever their colour or creed. Such an attitude would prevent her from seeing that the professional help offered to Clifford, including her counselling, might be so Westernised as to constitute cultural bias and prejudice.

Clifford's counsellor looks directly at her own racism. She has to look at her attitudes both inside and outside counselling. She distinguishes those occasions when her pessimism about outcome, her excessive politeness, and her inability to discuss racism at all have meant that her black clients have received less effective counselling than her white clients. She then relates these issues to Clifford's case and asks herself if he has not already become a 'problem' client in her mind even before counselling begins.

Then there is her attitude towards cultural differences. She considers carefully those parts of her own culture which she thinks are at variance with Clifford's and which will make acknowledgement, acceptance, and understanding of his culture difficult. Examples of differences between the two cultures might be:

- the relative significance of past or future events;
- the relative importance of traditional values;
- the differing obligations towards all members of the family;
- the use of scientific as opposed to intuitive ways of understanding events;
- the differing roles of women in the two cultures.

These differences may not all be pertinent to Clifford, but the counsellor will be concerned that they pose barriers between herself and her client. She will have to acknowledge these concerns and seek to increase her knowledge of her client's culture before counselling can begin.

COUNSELLORS' SKILLS

All counsellors are skilled people. Nelson-Jones (1988) considers that the most important skill of the counsellor is *good listening*. Second to this is communicating and facilitating understanding, managing problems, focusing on feeling, as well as being able to maintain and develop your skills. This book assumes that you have developed these general skills in counselling, and that you are seeking to develop these skills across cultures.

Sue et al. (1992) have more specifically organised thirty-one multicultural competencies, which they recommended should be used by US professional counselling bodies as part of their accreditation criteria. They have developed a three by three matrix of characteristics and dimensions. The characteristics are a) counsellor awareness of own assumptions, values and biases, b) understanding the world view of the culturally different client, and c) developing appropriate intervention strategies and techniques. Each of these characteristics has three dimensions: a) beliefs and attitudes, b) knowledge, and c) skills.

Black and minority ethnic counsellors are likely to be more culturally skilled than their white counterparts as they have already had to cope with an alien and hostile environment, and to learn its salient characteristics.

Counsellors who have not had this type of learning experience may therefore be *less* culturally skilled than their clients. Whatever your cultural background, you will need to ascertain:

- Your being able to anticipate and work with the fears that your clients bring with them, both about transcultural counselling and the counsellor.
- Your ability to listen accurately to the extensive information that clients across cultures offer.
- Your language skills, for instance, can you communicate in your client's language well enough to understand, or to speak simply, or to counsel your client?
- Your skill in deciding when and how to use interpreters when you cannot counsel in your client's language.
- Your non-verbal skills; for example, can you adopt the most appropriate gestures, greetings and body language for your client?
- Your ability to communicate and facilitate understanding across cultures.
- Your skill in managing your client's difficulties which occur within their cultural context.
- Your ability to focus on feelings expressed in ways unfamiliar to your culture.
- Your ability to interpret accurately the expression of strong feeling outside your own culture, for instance anger, fear, grief or joy.
- Your ability to recognise when a lack of expression of strong feeling by the client represents a cultural rather than an individual variation.
- Your skill in negotiating subjects that are taboo in the culture of the client whom you are counselling.
- Your skill in tackling the cultural and racial prejudices of your client, your client's culture, and society at large.
- Your skill in examining your own racial and cultural prejudices, and the ways they influence your attitudes and behaviour in counselling.
- Your skill in negotiating the effects of all these cultural prejudices and fears so that you can establish a more robust relationship.
- Your organisational skills, for example, deciding how and when to use community workers when you are not conversant with your client's culture.
- Your skill in involving the client's family and community networks appropriately.
- Your ability to maintain and develop your transcultural skills.

- Your skill in distinguishing individual differences and not generalising about a particular culture.

The issues of prejudice and racism are difficult and painful areas for both parties. Counsellors will therefore need to establish credibility *right at the start* with their clients in order to facilitate the process of dealing with cultural distance. The ability to negotiate the effects of prejudice will be used by counsellors not only before counselling starts, but also throughout the process.

First, the transcultural counsellor decides an appropriate time to introduce the subject of prejudice and racism during assessment. Secondly, the counsellor will tackle prejudice and racism from whatever source with conviction. Transcultural counsellors must be skilled in their manner as well as in their knowledge. A comparison can be drawn with the skills of the sexual counsellor who not only has theoretical knowledge of sexuality, but can also approach an intimate topic without embarrassment. In a transcultural setting, counselling skills include being comfortable about racism and cultural matters as well as having cultural information.

Finally, the counsellor working across cultures must be skilled enough to pick up, reflect and negotiate *explicitly* issues of prejudice. There are many degrees of racism and cultural prejudice. They range from the overtly hostile response, to the more subtle form of a patronising response. In practice the counsellor must be finely sensitised to personal as well as clients' prejudices, and monitor such behaviour as language, attitude and gesture.

Let us return to *Clifford,* and the cultural skills that his counsellor will want to use when counselling him. On the surface she speaks the same language as Clifford and may therefore assume that her communication skills will be adequate. But Clifford's English may be different from hers in a number of ways and she will have to be particularly attentive to his speech. A skilled counsellor will need to understand also that Clifford may prefer to be physically closer to the counsellor than she might expect.

The counsellor needs to know how and when an intimate or taboo subject can be introduced in a culturally appropriate way. A skilled counsellor may not know exactly all that is to happen in counselling. But she should be flexible and able to interpret non-verbal signs as important communications.

Clifford's counsellor needs to examine her own racism as well as be in touch with the racism that exists in the UK against him. For example, he

had to conform to English cultural standards in his rehabilitation programme: he was expected to role-play everyday conversations with other
disabled patients in a group. He withdrew from it, as he considered this to
be an embarrassing and undignified undertaking with strangers.

This and other such experiences upset Clifford, until he began to
demand what *he* wanted from counselling: namely, help with his sexual
problems. He then acquired the title of 'problem patient'. A skilled counsellor is able to acknowledge the effect of prejudice on Clifford's
experiences, anticipate how this will affect the expression of his problems, and work out a way of confronting these experiences in counselling.
More than this, Clifford's counsellor will need to approach these issues
early on in the counselling relationship. She will have to communicate with
confidence how much importance she attaches to his cultural experiences.

STATUS

All counsellors enjoy a position of power. In a transcultural setting, this
position is complicated by the discrepancy of status that exists between
cultures. The client's judgement of the counsellor's status will be influenced by a wide number of factors. What is more, this status is not static,
and will be reactive to the counselling process once it begins (see Lago and
Thompson, 1989).

As counsellors, you have a responsibility for your client, and for how
Western-style counselling is seen in your client's culture. Your 'diplomatic'
status applies equally when you are from another culture and are now
being counselled within a Western model, as in the case of *Rahima*.

In a setting where the counsellor is from the majority culture, and the
client from another culture, that counsellor will be seen as holding both
professional and cultural power. The counsellor is seen, rightly or
wrongly, as having more status and knowledge than her client, and the
influence of this perception will be felt throughout the entire relationship.
Difficulties will arise when you do not acknowledge your powerful status,
in the mistaken notion that if you deny its existence, your client will no
longer be influenced by it. On the contrary, it is only when, as counsellors,
you acknowledge this difference in status, that you and your clients can
tackle it and begin to change it.

These then, are the issues in practice:

- How your own cultural and ethnic status is perceived by the client.

- Whether or not your gender is likely to increase or decrease your status in your client's culture.
- Whether or not being older or younger than your client is important enough in your client's culture to affect your status.
- Whether or not your social and economic circumstances influence your status in your client's culture.
- Whether or not your status is altered for your client by your cultural and linguistic fluency.
- How your client's culture sees the role of counsellors.

As is the case in all counselling, *Fred's* counsellor is in a more powerful position than he is, as she has the skills, knowledge and expertise to help him with his problems. Furthermore, she is employed, and he is not. After his accident, he has been unable to return to work in the docks, and he regards all working people as enjoying a higher status than he does. She is also a professional, a role he views as being omnipotent.

However, there are some factors in his everyday living that are at odds with his counsellor's position of power. She is the same age as his children, and he sees young people as inexperienced and of low status. She is a woman, and in his world, women are rarely in positions of power over him. But most of all, she is Indian and speaks English with an educated accent, quite unlike other Asian people he has dealt with. In his neighbourhood, there is a great deal of prejudice and racism towards black people. There exists a large number of people from the Indian subcontinent who live in very poor economic conditions, and have little power in dealing with racism, both individual and institutional. Fred therefore sees Asian people as less powerful than himself.

When he meets his Indian counsellor for the first time, there is a reversal of power. The way that Fred copes with this discrepancy is to notice only her skin colour, which is the same as his doctor's. He then asks if the counsellor is the doctor's sister! He has already given status to his doctor, an Asian professional, in whom he has confidence. He wants the same for his counsellor and therefore relates her (literally) to his doctor.

CHOICES

When we considered clients' choices in counselling we referred to clients selecting culturally sensitised counsellors. In order to offer choice, counsellors need to exercise it, that is they need to develop their cultural knowledge in the many ways that have been outlined in this chapter.

This does not mean that counsellors have to know everything about all cultures. As we have said earlier, no single book could ever hope to offer you knowledge of that order. What is being referred to is an ongoing choice about how you approach any culture different from your own. This will demand a whole new way of thinking about your counselling, a way of enriching your skills with every new client, whatever their cultural origins.

You can choose to increase your information and experiences. You can choose to develop your skills. You can choose to use your personal and institutional resources. You can choose to change your attitudes and expectations. You can choose to examine your status with your client. Finally, you can choose to help increase your colleagues' knowledge of cultural and transcultural matters. Lago and Thompson (1996: 134), however, caution counsellors that enrolling on transcultural courses and having 'a generalised commitment may not be sufficient motivation to see them through the enormous challenges they will have to face'.

When seeing a particular client from another culture for the first time, therefore, you will need to consider the following choices:

- Whether or not you choose to work with clients from another culture.
- Whether or not you take awareness training about racism and cultural issues when offered.
- If such training is not available, whether or not you choose to establish such training programmes at work.
- Whether or not you choose to work with interpreters and community workers.
- Whether you accept transcultural clients because nobody wants them or because you have something positive to offer those clients.
- Whether or not you choose to develop your knowledge of other cultures outside your work.

In the case of *Rahima*, the counsellor has always chosen to work with clients from all cultures. She is herself in a transcultural setting, and is aware of the importance of counselling across cultures. She chooses to bring matters relating to cultural and racial differences at work to the attention of her colleagues. She regularly attends training programmes and tries to initiate these for other counsellors.

It therefore follows that this counsellor values working with people from different cultures: she does not choose only Indian clients. White counsellors in the neighbourhood project, on the other hand, do not choose to take on black clients for several reasons. First, clients outside the majority culture get 'dumped' on any black counsellor available. Secondly, black counsellors often feel a responsibility to take on black clients regardless of cultural distance, because their needs are disregarded by white counsellors. Thirdly, white counsellors are often fearful and inexperienced in working with black clients. Lastly, racism and prejudice erode the motivation of all counsellors to work transculturally.

When Rahima was referred to the neighbourhood project the counsellor chose to take her on. Although Asian, Rahima's background contrasts with her counsellor's. She was born and bred in a very different part of India, in a different time in Indian history, and with a different family lifestyle. Rahima is Muslim; her counsellor has a Hindu background. Rahima has lived in the UK for more than forty years, but has retained many of the cultural values with which she came to the UK. There are, however, cultural ties; she is an Indian woman living in the UK, and is a fellow-professional. In choosing to work transculturally, the counsellor has recognised these similarities and differences and elects to work with them all.

In conclusion, there is much that you as counsellors can do to prepare yourselves for counselling clients across cultures. We hope that you have been able to recognise the extent of your knowledge, both about your own culture and about others. Once you begin to examine critically your strengths and weaknesses in transcultural work, you will be ready to begin. Our next chapter will establish our four clients in the counselling process itself, and discuss ways of 'getting started'.

4

GETTING STARTED

Overview

In this chapter we shall look at our four clients as they meet their counsellors and consider good practice at the start of the counselling process. We discuss the issues of greetings and names and the differing forms of address within our clients' cultures. Then, we suggest how counsellors might establish their credibility in the eyes of their clients, and how boundaries are set by both parties. In addition, we shall examine assessment approaches from a cultural perspective and consider their appropriateness for clients across cultures. We shall also look at the different presentations of a problem across cultures. Finally, we shall consider the usefulness of goal setting for clients in another culture.

In our last two chapters, we described how the two parties in transcultural counselling bring their cultural knowledge to the relationship. In this chapter, our clients are going to meet their counsellors for the first time, and we shall see how their different kinds of cultural knowledge interact.

There is evidence (Lorion and Parron, 1985) to show that clients from minority ethnic groups do not start as well, and terminate counselling sooner than majority clients. It has been assumed that this was due to factors affecting the clients' expectations of counselling. Commonly cited was the notion that these clients 'medicalised' their problems, and expected instant cures. Clients from different cultures were described as using fewer verbal exchanges than majority clients, and as being less able and willing to form therapeutic relationships. Lago and Thompson (1996) note that effective white counsellors know that they 'think white' but are able 'to enter into the black person's world'.

In fact the evidence now shows that it is the counsellors' expectations that create this discrepancy right at the beginning of counselling. Lorion and Parron (1985) quote several studies that show that when counsellors have low expectations of counselling success with their ethnic clients, this will correlate highly with poor outcome in counselling. By implication, those counsellors who begin counselling disposed to being successful with such clients, do in fact keep their clients for longer with more effective outcome.

In practice, this means that you will need to be very careful in assessing your own beliefs about counselling in starting with a client from another culture. Such clients may have good reason for doubting the ability of their counsellors to help with their problems, and may express this in a number of ways.

First, clients may vote with their feet and end the counselling before it has even begun. It is all too easy to explain this in terms of the culturally different clients' resistance to counselling. It is more difficult, perhaps, for counsellors to look at their own negative expectations. Secondly, clients may sense their counsellors' low expectations of success, and blame themselves for this. They may then placate their counsellors by saying what they think the counsellor wants to hear.

Another possible way for white clients to express their doubts about their culturally different counsellors' abilities is to distort their statements. In this situation, clients perceive a power dissonance, that is counsellors have high status; black people do not. Clients from the dominant culture have to make sense of this by altering their perception. We will demonstrate this with Fred in his first meeting with his counsellor.

NAMES AND BEGINNINGS

As far back as 1979 Henley emphasised the importance of getting your clients' names right. She pointed out that every culture has its own naming system with its own logic. In Anglo-Saxon cultures, people have a given first name followed by an inherited family name. However, in Muslim cultures there is no such thing as an inherited family name; every member of a family has several. In order to comply with the Anglo-Saxon naming system, Muslim people give their last name as their surname, even though this may often be a personal name. Transcultural counsellors familiarise themselves with the naming convention of their client's culture, as well as the changes that have been made to conform with the majority culture.

In addition, you could learn both the spelling and pronunciation of your clients' names, and use the appropriate form of address. When counsellors perform this initial task with courtesy, it strikes a positive note with the client, and indicates care and consideration. It is helpful to write names down carefully. Ask your clients how they wish to be addressed. If you remain in any doubt, we suggest that you adopt a more formal manner of address, giving you the choice of becoming more familiar as the relationship develops.

Make clear how your own name is pronounced and how you wish to be addressed. Our own unusual names have highlighted the need to do this. If introductions are not made clearly and appropriately you may start counselling with a further cultural divide. Counsellors are seen as powerful people, and in that initial encounter, your clients are likely to feel overwhelmed and are unlikely to correct you. Take the trouble to get names right and begin to establish credibility.

In *Rahima's* case, her counsellor knows her age before they meet for the first time. She also knows that in Bengali culture, an older person expects to be addressed formally as a sign of respect. The fact that the counsellor is culturally close to her increases this obligation.

Counsellor: (in Bengali) Salaam-walai-kum.
Rahima: (in Bengali) Walai-kum-salaam. (in English) How nice to be greeted in a familiar way!

At this point, the counsellor introduces herself, and her role as counsellor to her client. She then moves on to establishing how she will address her client.

Counsellor: How would you like me to call you?
Rahima: I'd like to be called Mrs. B . . .

In the above exchange, the counsellor establishes an immediate rapport with her client by greeting her client in Bengali. Although the counsellor is not fully fluent in Bengali, she knows that this small consideration will set a positive tone to the beginning of the relationship. Further, having introduced herself to Rahima, the counsellor takes the trouble to ascertain how Rahima wishes to be addressed. Rahima starts with a more formal title, but this will change as the relationship becomes more intimate and established.

In *Fred's* case, for instance, we already know what his attitudes were to the Asian families in his own neighbourhood, and how he has had to adjust his views when meeting his Asian counsellor for the first time. His prejudices about other cultures and races go deep, as does his distrust of anything with which he is not familiar. His feelings of hostility and suspicion towards his counsellor are modified into what he believes is an acceptable exchange:

Counsellor: Your doctor has asked me to see you about some of the difficulties you've been having recently.

Fred: Oh, you must be his sister; he's a very nice man, isn't he?

Counsellor: Yes, he is very nice, but I'm not related to him. He is a colleague of mine, and we work closely together.

Fred: I didn't realise.

Counsellor: Well, now that we've cleared up that misunderstanding, why don't you tell me a little bit about yourself and what's been happening recently?

Fred: I don't know how much you know about living in East London. I've been here all my life, and I've seen many different people come here.

Counsellor: Tell me about them.

The counsellor considers Fred's initial error about her identity and understands why this has been expressed in this way. She informs him that she is not related to his doctor in a non-judgemental manner, but she is aware that Fred's words reflect a racist attitude that will need to be tackled when the relationship is established more firmly. White people commonly associate racism with aggressive or abusive behaviour; in fact it comes in many forms. A white counsellor would never have been 'lumped' together with a white colleague by Fred. In relating his counsellor to his doctor, Fred is unable to acknowledge her identity or individuality.

When he is invited to talk about himself, Fred refers only to his external world and explicitly challenges his counsellor's knowledge about this world. His reference to 'many different people' seems to be a comment about the cultural and racial distance between Fred and his counsellor. His counsellor makes note of these processes but cannot explore his feelings so early in counselling. There is not as yet a safe enough relationship for this to be discussed.

Mathilde's counsellor is the same age as her and is culturally close. She could presume familiarity but instead asks Mathilde how she likes to be addressed. Mathilde gives her first name and the counsellor does the same. Nevertheless, when speaking to her in French the counsellor uses the more formal pronoun 'vous' for 'you', rather than the 'tu' form. The use of language here allows the counsellor and her client to maintain some distance from each other.

Mathilde's knowledge about her counsellor before getting started is greater than Fred's. She knows that her counsellor is a woman and that she speaks French. Her counsellor knows in advance that Mathilde has experienced a very difficult period of time in England. She also knows that many French people find English people to be insensitive, stubborn and prejudiced towards the French. What she does not know is the strength of Mathilde's concerns.

When Mathilde meets her counsellor for the first time, she worries about her counsellor expressing intolerance, and tests the water by asking:

Mathilde: Can we speak French all the time? It makes me feel less like a foreigner.

Counsellor: Of course we can. Tell me about being a Frenchwoman living in this country.

Mathilde: I feel so out of place here. I was meant to have my baby in France, and instead he was born here. I find it hard to work out the system here. Everything at home is so much simpler for the mother. Here you have to go through so much bureaucracy to get the help you want.

Counsellor: It sounds like you've had a difficult time. How would you like me to help you?

Mathilde: I just need to know that there's somebody around who understands me. I tried talking to my husband, John, lots of times about how desperate I feel, but he doesn't understand what I'm talking about.

Counsellor: I see. You must be feeling very much on your own. Let's take things one at a time. We've got an opportunity now to sort things out.

In this exchange, Mathilde's counsellor responds immediately to her request to speak in French. She also uses the term 'Frenchwoman', rather than 'foreigner'. In doing so, the counsellor positively values her client's cultural origin.

Mathilde refers to her problems with the outside world but, very significantly, mentions a communication difficulty with her husband as well. Mathilde is taking a risk here, as she has only just met her counsellor. However, a good rapport has been established by the counsellor's willingness to use French, and unconditional acceptance of her client's difficulties. The counsellor appreciates that there is a lot of material to cover, and sets a structure to their work by suggesting an order.

Clifford's first meeting with his counsellor does not run as smoothly as the counsellor would like it to. She introduces herself and mentions the rehabilitation staff who have referred him.

> *Clifford*: I'm not interested in what they have to say about me. They
> don't understand me. That's why I asked to see somebody else.
> *Counsellor*: I see. You sound quite angry about them. Why don't we
> start by your telling me in your own words what you see as the
> problem?
> *Clifford*: Are you going to tell them what I say to you?
> *Counsellor*: Not if you don't want me to. I do have to tell them that I've
> seen you today, but I don't have to give them any details.
> *Clifford*: Okay. Well the main thing is that I have a sexual problem, and
> it's making life at home difficult. I know there's other things, but
> that's what's worrying me now.
> *Counsellor*: Fine, let's talk about that.

In this first meeting, the counsellor unwittingly refers to the tense relationship between Clifford and the hospital staff. He responds by expressing his anger very directly, which takes the counsellor aback. She had prepared herself for a gradual introduction to Clifford. Her own agenda consisted of asking him about his cultural background and early life. Instead, she is confronted with the very source of his pain and frustration.

The counsellor then attempts to shift the focus back to her client's account, but he is not yet ready to let go of his irritation. He challenges her on the issue of confidentiality, and she responds with a truthful answer, but one which has a collusive element in it. Clifford is able to accept this as a basis for starting counselling, and immediately moves into the area of sexual difficulties.

ESTABLISHING YOUR CREDENTIALS

Some counsellors introduce themselves and explain their role and function to their clients at the outset of counselling. We believe that this is of particular value in a transcultural setting. The very idea of counselling as an approach to problem solving is itself culture-bound. Clients from other cultures need the opportunity to absorb this idea, and to put questions to their counsellor while getting started.

There are other issues that need to be tackled in establishing your credentials. If you are a counsellor culturally close to your client, the client may fear loss of confidentiality to be a barrier to getting started. Transculturally aware counsellors can anticipate this issue, and reassure their clients that they will respect confidences, and that counselling is in no way comparable to socialising within the community.

Counselling has evolved primarily in European and American cultures. Katz (1985) lists some of the components of counselling and very clearly demonstrates how these are intimately linked to the values and beliefs of white culture. Examples of these components are individualism, action orientation, use of status and expertise, Western-style talk therapy, self-disclosure, and goal orientation. Katz (1985: 617) concludes that 'theories develop from individual perspectives, experiences and practices, all of which are embedded in a particular cultural context'. We shall return to the effects of these cultural components on the counselling relationship in Chapter 6.

The establishment of counsellor credibility is an essential prerequisite to getting started in counselling. Sue and Sue (1990) refer to 'counsellor credibility' as having two distinct components. The first of these is an ability variable, which they call expertness. The second is a motivational variable, called trustworthiness. They suggest that the counsellor's formal qualifications may not be enough, especially as counsellors may be from an institution that their clients have already judged as being racist. They argue that counsellors may have to prove their expertise in practice rather than through formal qualification. Counsellors' trustworthiness in the eyes of their clients will play a critical role not only in establishing credentials, but also when clients have to make decisions about self-disclosure. We shall pursue this area later in the book.

Different cultures have different ways of coping with distress; transcultural counsellors undertake to find out more about these coping mechanisms and adjust their method accordingly. This is how counsellors can establish their credentials. Let us look at our clients.

In *Rahima's* case, her son insisted that her family could do no more for their mother, and that 'professional' help be sought for her. In this context, counselling may be a difficult idea for the client to accept. Rahima needs and wants help but she expresses mixed feelings about counselling under these conditions.

> *Rahima*: I've only ever spoken to my late brother about problems in the family. I'm glad you're Indian, but I'm very upset that my son has sent me to see you.
>
> *Counsellor*: I appreciate how you must be feeling. But you're here now, which suggests that you do want to talk to somebody. It will get better as we go along.
>
> *Rahima*: Maybe so, but how much of what I tell you will get back to my son, Farooq?
>
> *Counsellor*: Nothing without your wanting it to.

Rahima sees the use of an outsider as a sign of failure. This picture is further complicated by the fact that Rahima seems enthusiastic about an Indian counsellor. Her counsellor tackles this ambivalence at the beginning of counselling by referring to it, and discussing with Rahima how difficult it must be to come into this situation. She answers specific questions about confidentiality and the involvement of her family in counselling.

Fred's case is somewhat different. He has always turned to male friends, and male members of his own family, when he has had problems. He has hardly discussed his difficulties with his wife. The only time he has used outside help was on medical or legal grounds. Thus the notion of a complete stranger, particularly a black woman, discussing his most private feelings with him outside his home, is quite foreign to him. The counsellor, therefore, will have to reiterate her role and purpose in many ways.

When starting counselling, Fred copes by reverting to a very physical description of his problems, and avoiding eye contact with his counsellor. She responds by reassuring him:

> *Counsellor*: It must seem very strange talking about this with an outsider.
>
> *Fred*: Yes, I feel I've been put on the spot.
>
> *Counsellor*: I can understand that. But you've already begun to share your problems with me, and I know it will get easier for you over time.

Here we see that Fred needs encouragement throughout the period of getting started. His counsellor senses that this is because of her cultural distance from him, and responds by reminding him of how much he has already started to share with her. Although he avoids eye contact with her, she continues to look directly at him, and enables him to persevere.

In conclusion, counsellors working across cultures have many tasks in establishing their credentials with their clients. But they need also to be careful of overemphasising cultural or racial factors to the exclusion of other variables. Your client can and will reject you for all kinds of reasons including your culture. You may be the 'wrong' age, gender or profession, and you will need to equip yourself to tackle all these resistances when starting counselling. Your cultural knowledge and skills will enable you to examine, anticipate and deal with prejudice whenever it presents itself.

BOUNDARIES

As we pointed out in Chapter 1, the beginnings of any counselling deal with the establishment of boundaries, whether implicit or explicit. Both parties bring their cultural knowledge, and their ideas about the nature and purpose of counselling, to the relationship. Boundaries are established by mutual consent and agreement, but it is the counsellor who remains in the more powerful position of determining where, when and under what conditions counselling sessions occur. Furthermore, counsellors can determine the content and approach used in counselling, even though these may be discussed with the client.

In a transcultural setting, clients may be unfamiliar with a notion of boundary-setting when getting started. For example, the use of strict time-keeping is a Western practice, which may pose unrealistic demands on clients from other cultures. The counsellor also has control over the physical boundaries of counselling. The choice of room, the furniture and decor, the location and distancing of seats, lighting, permission to smoke, all constitute boundaries that will influence how counselling gets started. The physical environment can be a powerful statement of your transcultural viewpoint. For example, if you choose to have pictures or photographs on the wall, it is more welcoming to have those which depict people from different cultures, or show different parts of the world.

Non-verbal behaviour is also part of boundary-setting. The manner of greeting, including handshakes, smiling, physical gestures and proximity immediately sets the tone for the session. During counselling itself, all these, as well as silences, bodily orientation, touching and your facial expression will set the limits of the relationship.

Boundaries are also set by verbal behaviour. Your first utterance to your client may decide which language you will use for the rest of counselling. You need to be clear about whether or not you have the skill to continue working in another language.

Counsellors may transgress boundaries by posing culturally inappropriate or intrusive questions to their client, who may then decline to reply. This in turn may be interpreted by the counsellor as resistance, and becomes part of the problem in the counsellor's mind. An example of an inappropriate first question by a white counsellor trying to put a black client at ease is, 'which country do you come from?' If the counsellor does not know whether the client is British-born or not, such a question can be distancing and racist when getting started. Only when the counsellor has established trust or when the client has raised the subject of culture, can the topic of the client's background be discussed sensitively.

Clients too can start counselling by making statements or gestures that are culturally inappropriate or intrusive. The culturally unskilled counsellor may respond in such a way that the client feels rejected, and they both flounder. An example of how to manage such a situation is shown in the case below.

Clifford gets started in counselling by pulling his chair to a few inches from his counsellor's. While he is speaking, he regularly puts his hand on the counsellor's leg, and occasionally slaps her knee. In this instance, the counsellor could push her chair back and reestablish the boundaries that existed in her mind before counselling had started. But she recognises Clifford's need for a sign of warmth and friendship. Although she perceives his approach as inappropriate, she decides to accept this contact. However, she does not volunteer any similar gestures in return, as she herself does not feel comfortable doing this. On subsequent occasions when she knows she is seeing Clifford, she arranges her chair by her desk in such a way that Clifford cannot put himself quite so close to her. Boundaries are thus established physically for the moment, but will be subject to change within the counselling process.

Rahima's counsellor has to set psychological boundaries. Rahima comes to the counsellor, very worried about her younger daughter's liaison with a white man. She immediately begins to ask about her counsellor's personal relationships with men.

Rahima: Do you have an English boyfriend?

Counsellor: You'd like to know about my personal life.

Rahima: Yes, it would help me to know what you think about relationships with Englishmen.

Counsellor: I can appreciate that you want to know what my views are, but what matters is how *you* feel about it.

Rahima: Yes, but I would still feel more comfortable if you would tell me.

Counsellor: I see. But the way in which I can help you deal with your difficulties is by remaining objective.

Rahima wants to know whether her counsellor, who is of a similar age and appearance to her daughter, has a Westernised lifestyle that will influence the counsellor's way of working with Rahima. The counsellor sets the limits for counselling in the following ways:

- First, she explicitly accepts her client's need to find out more about her counsellor and her cultural beliefs.
- Secondly, she reminds her client of the need to focus on *her* (that is the client's) problems.
- Thirdly, the counsellor explains that telling the client her cultural beliefs is not going to help them resolve her problems in an objective manner.

The counsellor accepts Rahima's concerns without necessarily agreeing with her need to know about her private life. This acceptance goes some way to reassuring the client, and to establishing working boundaries in the therapeutic relationship.

ASSESSMENT

In our work as clinical psychologists, we are accustomed to assessing the behaviour, attitudes and abilities of our clients through the use of precise tests and methodologies. Most psychometric tests, however, have been standardised only on ethnic majority populations, and could not be used reliably with clients from other cultures.

Historically, some researchers (Jensen, 1981) have looked at psychological differences between racial groups, and concluded that there were innate differences between them. These studies contributed to a climate of opinion where black people were judged to be intellectually inferior. The other side of the coin was that IQ tests were found to be unreliable and culturally biased for many ethnic groups. For these reasons, psychometric testing is a daunting undertaking in a transcultural setting. Writing about assessment across cultures, MacCarthy (1988: 130) concludes: 'the use of standardized instruments generally raises complex difficulties in cross-cultural assessment and cannot substitute for face-to-face, culturally-sensitive interviewing.' Butcher et al. (1998) list factors requiring special consideration in assessment which include: language limitations, cultural differences, motivational differences, different ideas of abnormality and different interpersonal expectations on the part of the client.

Bavington and Majid (1986) and Fernando (1995) refer to the risk of bias in the assessment of psychiatric disorders across cultures. They draw attention to the fact that the clients' presentation is affected by their perceptions and expectations of the setting. For example, they quote Asian patients who believe that the doctor wants to know about physical symptoms rather than their emotional state. Thus, the two parties have different agendas and fail to achieve an accurate assessment. Whether you are a counsellor or a psychiatrist, working across cultures demands that you spend time with your client in clarifying the purpose of assessment.

As counsellors working across cultures, the assessment of our clients includes an emphasis on the establishment of a relationship characterised by respect and understanding. This may involve members of the client's family and community in the assessment, even more than is usual with Western counselling. We have found the great value of being flexible in this respect in our work in East London. One of us (d'Ardenne, 1986b) was referred a Bangladeshi couple with a sexual problem, who arrived with a grandmother, two uncles, an aunt and a small baby. The assessment was done with all the family making a contribution, and in fact helping the couple in their home assignments, by providing them with time, privacy and babysitting.

We also believe that assessment in a transcultural setting has a very particular purpose. Lonner and Sondberg (1985: 199) propose that the goal of assessment here 'is to minimise ethnocentrism and maximise useful and culturally appropriate information'. They argue that the culturally encapsulated counsellor must shift position and find a common framework for both cultures. Transcultural assessment must identify and describe the problem and develop the means of resolving it in a way acceptable to both parties.

In practice, then, as a counsellor you must remain very flexible about assessment techniques, and use opportunities as and when they present themselves. Full allowance must be made for the decrease in reliability and validity of any standardised procedures in the context of transcultural counselling.

PRESENTATION

The counsellor has many types of information available: there is the factual side of what the client is saying and there is the manner in which the problem is expressed. We cannot emphasise enough that there are different cultural taboos about the expression of strong feeling in a wide variety of contexts.

For example, Triandis (1985) has described some major dimensions of culture that will affect how your clients from other cultures express themselves when they come for counselling. He looks at collectivist and individualist cultures and notes that, in practice, clients from the former lay greater emphasis on factors such as age, gender and religion. They look for their own cultural group's norms and authority, and they are concerned with group loyalty and cohesion. Clients from individualist cultures, on the other hand, are less sensitive to the views of others. They are more concerned with personal ethics and comfort, and select their acceptable behaviours from beyond their own cultural group.

Similarly, he considers 'tight', highly regulated cultures and compares them to 'loose', heterogeneous cultures. In practice, clients from the former observe social norms with great care when presenting their problems at the start of counselling. Clients from tight cultures place greater emphasis on rules of behaviour and conformity with their own family, religion, race or nationality.

Clients from 'contact' cultures are distinguished from 'no-contact' cultures by seeking close interpersonal space in the counselling room, by touching their counsellor, by direct eye contact and by speaking loudly.

Different culture clients will vary in what they select as being a problem, and in the choice they make of people to help them. You will need to acquaint yourselves with these major differences in world view if you are to show cultural sensitivity in assessing your clients. Here is a practical example. Early on in counselling, *Clifford* pulls up his chair, sits down, thumps the table and stares at the wall, saying:

Let me tell you the problem as I see it – I have been growing
weaker for some time and I can't tell you people about it.
Everybody's been telling me what the matter is with me, but I
know why things aren't working, and I just want to set the record
straight!
Counsellor: I'm here to listen to whatever you have to say. If you want
to talk about the sex problem, that's okay with me.

His counsellor could have put aside this announcement and led him back
to history taking. In doing this, she would have denied him the chance of
describing his sexual problem in a way that was culturally appropriate to
him. We have already spoken about his coming to be counselled by a
white woman. If the counsellor investigates his problem by asking precise
and explicit details about his sexual behaviour, he might withdraw.

As it is, his counsellor recognises the full significance of his statement,
and makes an immediate decision to respond directly to his opening dec-
laration. She provides him with the opportunity to ventilate his feelings,
and directs her questions towards the sexual difficulties that he has mentioned. She knows she can eventually obtain a more detailed history from
Clifford, but it is not essential at this stage. Clifford needs to have his
problems assessed on his own terms.

Since Freud and the development of psychoanalytic theory, great
importance has been placed on assessing the history of the client as the
first step towards solving the problem. The exploration and interpretation
of past events as a means of dealing with the present is not unique to the
Western world, but neither is it a universally held view.

You should inform your clients of the reasons for history taking, and
explain to them how this assists the process of getting started. For example, *Rahima's* counsellor asks her for background information about her
early life and marriage. She replies by laughing and saying:

You don't want to know about that – it all happened long before you
were even born!
Counsellor: I know that these are important events in your life. It would
help me to understand you better if you could share something of
your past with me.
Rahima: Yes, but where shall we begin?
Counsellor: Let's go back as far as you can remember.

The client genuinely cannot see the relevance of events forty years ago on her present predicament. By a process of gentle questioning, the counsellor enables Rahima to recognise the importance of the past in shaping the present. She gradually accepts this approach and begins exploring her early experiences and relationships with her counsellor.

The consequences of the counsellor assessing Rahima's problems sensitively and carefully, taking as much time as she needs, means that her counselling starts well, and the counsellor is able to establish her credentials. Rahima is more likely to return the following week and develop a trusting and well-founded relationship with her counsellor. In our experience, if assessment is not mutually discussed and acceptable, then the client will either not return, or will develop resistance towards the counsellor, which the counsellor may not be able to anticipate or deal with.

In conclusion, there are as many different types of assessment in counselling as there are schools of counselling. We have proposed a transcultural theme in assessment across cultures that makes it more reliable and appropriate.

GOALS

Throughout this chapter, we have examined those processes at the start of counselling that are likely to be affected by cultural issues. When assessment has been completed, the counsellor and client should have enough information to begin to make therapeutic choices. At this stage, both parties may still be separated culturally about the purpose of counselling, and it may be useful to discuss *goal setting*.

Of course, goal setting is itself a culturally determined activity. Katz (1985) actually refers to it as an example of a Western, 'rational' procedure that counsellors use in order to persuade themselves and their clients that they will be able to recognise therapeutic change in counselling. Counsellors may need to introduce it as an activity unfamiliar to their client's everyday life, but which will help both of them to work together better. Setting goals with individual clients, whatever their cultural origin, will be a very rewarding task, and one which we will describe in more detail in Chapter 7.

Nelson-Jones (1988) has listed the advantages and disadvantages of setting goals and suggested that counsellors evaluate both the individual and cultural appropriateness of some of the goals drawn up in a counselling contract. On the positive side, he suggests that goal setting at the start of counselling establishes:

- a 'clarity' of focus – clients can concentrate on an agreed objective;
- an 'increase in motivation' – clients have concrete goals to work towards;
- 'increased persistence' – clear goals mean that clients will persevere with their therapeutic tasks;
- 'increased action planning' – clients will be encouraged to change their behaviour, rather than merely talk about it.

On the negative side, Nelson-Jones (1988) suggests that goal setting may:

- 'create dependence' – given the opportunity, clients may expect the counsellor to set goals for them;
- 'be too mechanistic' – goals may be set too soon and too simplistically, and may even damage the counselling relationship;
- 'place too much pressure' – unrealistic expectations may develop and lead to a sense of failure if not achieved;
- 'represent helpers' needs' – the counsellor's own need to get results may be represented in the goals that are set.

In practice, *Clifford's* counsellor gets started by discussing goal setting with him. It is true that he has already experienced a highly structured rehabilitation programme. His therapists have also attempted to define his progress in concrete stages so that he could monitor change for himself. But the result has been that Clifford complains increasingly of 'being pushed' to do things, and argues with the hospital staff about whether or not he has agreed to undertake them in the first place.

In this case, the decision has to be made about whether it is goal setting that has proved to be counter-therapeutic, or whether it has been that the goals have not been suited to the specific needs of the client. Clifford's counsellor asks him more about this, and it becomes clear to both of them that he wants another chance to work in this way, but that he would prefer to have more input into setting the goals. In particular, he wants graded stages nearer his own pace. It appears that Clifford has never felt fully consulted about the goals of treatment established in his rehabilitation programme, where he feels he has been bullied. Indeed, his therapist has explained that it is a necessary requirement of her therapy that her patients feel bullied! Clifford describes how he had ideas about his own progress that he had tried to express, but he believes that his previous therapists expected more of him. He became discouraged and, somewhat perversely, set out to prove that he could not meet their expectations.

In conclusion, our four clients have brought very differing needs to the initial counselling session. We have helped all of them to get started in counselling. In the next chapter, we shall consider a common language between clients and their counsellors and ways in which better communication can be fostered in a transcultural setting.

5

A COMMON LANGUAGE

Overview

In this chapter we shall be showing how a common language can be found across cultures, and shall again use our four clients to highlight the issues of communication. We will look at non-verbal communication and consider its most significant aspects. Next, we examine the prominence of standard English in Western culture, and the way this discriminates against speakers of other forms of English. Then, bilingualism as a skill in counselling will be looked at, together with the issues that occur when working in more than one language, in particular the importance of linguistic equivalence. We shall then suggest the best ways in which interpreters can be used in counselling and, finally, demonstrate how racist values are sustained through the use of words whose meanings have changed over time.

Truax and Carkhuff (1967: 25) note that all theories of psychotherapy stress '. . . that for the therapist to be helpful he must be accurately empathic, be "with" the client, be understanding, or *grasp the patient's meaning*' [emphasis added]. They further specify (Truax and Carkhuff, 1967: 25) 'the therapist's ability to *communicate* [emphasis added] empathic understanding and unconditional positive regard' as being necessary and sufficient conditions for therapeutic change.

This core of effective communication is common to all counselling but clearly raises very particular issues for the culturally skilled counsellor. In the first instance a common language must be found. As counsellors, we all select and adjust our mode of speech to what we perceive as the client's intellectual, social and emotional level. We would probably speak differently to a professor of law than a teenage rock star. An effective counsellor assumes responsibility for finding a shared language with the client.

Similarly, in a cross-cultural setting, we need to select and adjust our mode of speech sensitively to our clients' needs. Some counsellors have interpreted this to mean shouting at their clients – a practice we do not endorse! Transcultural counsellors use clear, precise language, and request feedback from the client as to whether communication is effective. Communication occurs at many levels: linguistic, grammatical, gestural, postural, attitudinal and conceptual. In this chapter we shall cover many of these.

NON-VERBAL COMMUNICATION ACCOMPANYING SPEECH

There is evidence (Argyle, 1981) to show that therapists can greatly improve their effectiveness with clients if they pay attention to clients' non-verbal cues. These include eye contact, gestures, proximity to the client, bodily orientation, facial expression, head movements and bodily contact. Furnham and Bochner (1986) have shown that in a transcultural setting, people from different cultures have different ways of:

- sending and receiving information;
- expressing their wishes and commands;
- demonstrating feeling.

When two people of differing cultures meet, they will need to negotiate their varied modes of communication. Furnham and Bochner (1986) further point out that this task becomes more difficult when the two parties share the *same* language. They argue that this is because the language similarities may mask differences that exist in their cultures. For example, the American who travels to London may succumb to a false sense of being at home when she hears a language familiar to her. She speaks effusively with the proprietor of a wine bar, who interprets this behaviour as flirtatious by his cultural standards. Unless one or both of them negotiate their messages accurately, there is likely to be misunderstanding. The main ways in which non-verbal signals assist communication are by:

- elaborating on what is said;
- providing feedback from listener to sender;
- giving messages about when it is time to speak or listen (Furnham and Bochner, 1986).

Furnham and Bochner (1986) use the example of how Arabs and Latin Americans have high levels of mutual gaze when compared to Europeans. Our experience, however, tells us that the picture is more complex: your client's mood, self-esteem and unfamiliarity with counselling will influence eye gaze. In practical terms, this would mean that counsellors seeing a client from these cultures may need to adjust their own gaze accordingly to establish non-verbal congruence.

In addition Henley (1979) points out the critical role of feedback. She makes the important observation that non-verbal behaviours may provide you with information about how much language has been understood (or not) in the interview. She cites the following examples: a glazed expression, a change of behaviour, for example, shifting in chair, a fixed smile, a look of embarrassment, or a repeated 'yes'.

In general it seems that facial expressions and gaze are more important in the communication of feeling than spatial behaviour. Transcultural counsellors learn the particular rules and conventions of the culture of their client and ensure that these are reciprocated in the counselling process.

Furnham and Bochner (1986) also refer to evidence about members of a dominant section in a particular society. For example, white nurses in South Africa experience fewer problems in meeting society, as measured in a social situations questionnaire, than their black counterparts. This is because white people had more opportunities to learn mainstream socially skilled acts, whereas black people were separated from the dominant sectors of society.

In our experience in East London, transcultural clients from a less powerful section of society are doubly disadvantaged in communication. Their right to be understood is affected in two ways:

- Their first language is other than English. They are therefore unable to communicate outside their own community and influence their wider world.
- Racism affords them fewer opportunities to learn the unspoken rules and conventions that accompany the English language.

You will be more effective counsellors if you understand and are sympathetic to these disadvantages. Furthermore, you can help your clients by valuing them and their culture enough to learn their major rules and conventions accompanying speech. Good examples of these are:

- learning non-verbal rules governing 'please' and 'thank you';
- the appropriate volume with which you speak;
- etiquette, for example, rules concerning social invitations;
- values about time-keeping.

In the case of *Rahima* she invites her counsellor to dinner as a means of thanking her and consolidating her relationship with her. Her counsellor replies positively but carefully that she is very touched by her thoughtfulness. The counsellor smiles and maintains steady eye-contact with Rahima as she explains that her role does not permit her to accept such an offer. The warmth of the counsellor's non-verbal signals accompanying her refusal assures Rahima that she is still accepted by her counsellor.

ENGLISH IN ITS MANY FORMS

English is a world language (Sinclair, 1995) with many spoken forms. We assume that our readers have no difficulty in following us in what we judge to be 'standard' written English. The spoken word, however, is more subject to variation. Richmond (1986) observes that if children's language differs from standard English pronounced in the accent of a white middle-class southerner, it is inadequate, inappropriate or incorrect. English-speaking counsellors expect their clients to share their manner of speech. When they do not, counsellors may devalue their clients, either by believing that they are intellectually slow or that they are uneducated.

Black clients who speak another form of English, for example, are even less likely to be understood by their counsellors than those who speak another language and require interpreters. Sue (1981) quotes a lively example of a black adolescent in New York who is totally misunderstood by his counsellor, who is unable to understand his street talk and takes every word uttered quite literally.

Also in the United States, Thomas and Sillen (1972) noted that language differences among black clients were judged as deficits by social scientists and educators. Black youngsters were also seen as having restricted opportunities for cognitive development because they had 'restricted' language forms. Thomas and Sillen quote early work that challenges the stereotype of verbally destitute lower-class black children. On the contrary, they found the language and abstract thinking of these children were fully developed in their own form of English. What the children had to contend with was English speakers who did not understand their form of English, and judged it as inferior to their own.

Wong (1986: 121) makes the important point that Patois and Creole are languages that developed because they were, '. . . necessary for intra-community communication that excluded others. The language became at once a source of pride as well as a barrier behind which the community survived'. In practice, transcultural counsellors who speak to their black clients in 'standard' English will appreciate why that barrier exists and respect the reasoning behind it.

Milner (1983) states that young Caribbean children living in the UK are frequently corrected for speaking 'bad' English, even though their English is grammatically consistent and culturally correct. No assistance is given to them to learn a form of English which is new to them. Instead they are castigated as 'poor' speakers and are seen as cognitively impaired. This experience is carried into their adult lives and may be reawakened when they meet the 'standard' English-speaking counsellor. In practice, then, we are faced with a situation where any client who speaks an alternative form of English, will often be disadvantaged by prejudice.

Clifford does not speak standard English. He speaks with an accent, vocabulary and sentence structure that reflects his own Nigerian culture. English is his first language, but when he first comes to see his counsellor he faces someone who speaks 'standard' English and who may judge him, as others have done, to be uneducated or unintelligent.

Counsellors with cultural sensitivity will appreciate that 'standard' English is not spoken by all, and that it may indeed impose an additional barrier to client-counsellor communication. Further, they will be looking at their own prejudices about language, and allowing for them when listening to alternative forms of English.

Of course language disadvantage is not only experienced by people from another culture. Class and education are just as likely to produce alternative forms of English which promote prejudice among listeners. We have already spoken in Chapter 2 about Fred's initial discomfort in speaking with a Cockney accent to a black, educated counsellor. He is particularly sensitive to people whom he sees as 'better' educated than himself, especially when he believes that they are in some way judging his behaviour. Our contention is that Fred may have suffered in this respect, but in a different way from a black person. People from other cultures suffer additional barriers to communication because of prejudice about their colour, their culture *and* their language.

WORKING ACROSS LANGUAGES

In Chapters 2 and 3 we described clients' and counsellors' cultural skills including language. Clients whose first language is not English have to learn the majority language as a matter of necessity. When they approach an authority such as the social services, health services or the police, they *have* to communicate on the terms of that authority. What is more, that communication often concerns vital and distressing material. Even people working in their first language might find this information difficult to communicate clearly.

In counselling across cultures, these same factors still apply. The client approaches the counsellor – an authority figure – for help with concerns that are distressing, vital and very personal. The counsellor rarely assumes responsibility for learning the client's language, for finding a common language, or even for learning about the problems that clients face in communicating in another language.

Henley (1979) makes the point that even when clients speak excellent English, everyday stress reduces their fluency. Similarly, clients who have little English may lose it altogether when exposed to similar stress. This is not a phenomenon peculiar to the English tongue. We all lose our skill in a second language when fatigued, stressed or angry.

When clients have no choice about language, they are distanced from expressing themselves fully. If clients are counselled in their first language they gain easier access to important cultural and familial experiences.

Transcultural counsellors, working across languages, understand the limitations imposed on their clients by this lack of choice. In practice, this may mean that counsellors need to take longer to explore significant feelings and experiences. A way of doing this is to approach a particular topic in a number of different ways in order to help the client elaborate more clearly.

Furnham and Bochner (1986) consider that the acquisition of the majority language is the single most important aspect of integration in a majority culture. Inability to do this, they suggest, usually leads to decreased social mobility, increased ghetto living and increased disruption between parents and children.

In our view the picture is more complex than this; language is a necessary but not sufficient condition for increased social change. The xeno-phobic attitudes of the majority culture ensure that members from other cultures are 'kept in their place'. Counsellors from the dominant culture must recognise that their attitudes are part of their cultural inheritance. Effective counsellors are those who are aware of the many subtle forms in which this inheritance is revealed.

Bilingualism

Counsellors and clients who are bilingual have an additional resource which enriches transcultural counselling. They have a greater choice in terms of language, as well as insight into the difficulties of moving from one given language to another.

Although local community groups in the UK use bilingualism as a resource, there have been no nationwide attempts to harness counsellors' language resources. There does, however, exist a training programme in the US (Pedersen, 1985, 1988) whose objective is to prepare culturally effective counsellors to work with bilingual, multicultural populations. It has produced bilingual counsellors in English and Spanish, Portuguese, Chinese, Italian and Creole. In the UK, there have also been attempts to recruit and train bilingual counsellors for specific communities (Mahtani and Marks, 1994).

In our case examples, *Rahima's* counsellor is learning to speak Bengali and uses it occasionally with her, when she wants to bring a cultural dimension to their communication. Rahima is herself bilingual and appre-ciates the effort and commitment made by her counsellor to establish a common language between them. Her counsellor is already bilingual in English and Hindi and understands some of the advantages and chal-lenges of working across languages. Her learning of Bengali has given a unique insight into Rahima's culture which has helped to enhance the counselling process.

Linguistic Equivalence

Our clients cannot enjoy the right to be understood unless the English lan-guage has some degree of equivalence with their own. By this we mean that there has to be a degree of correspondence of meaning when trans-lating from one language to another. English is a very rich language for the expression of mood and feeling. However the language is limited in other ways.

For example, English is more limited in defining family relationships when compared with languages from family-centred cultures. Just as the Laplander has over twenty different words for something as important as snow, so Hindi speakers have separate words for family relations. In English there are only the words 'aunt' and 'uncle'. In Hindi, there are different words for your mother's sister and brother-in-law, and your mother's brother and sister-in-law. The same is true for your father's relatives. There are thus four different words for 'aunt' and four different words for 'uncle'. In counselling a client from this family-centred culture, the counsellor working only in English is limited in her understanding of the subtlety of family relationships. By asking questions and using many words, the counsellor may be able to identify which of her client's aunts is being referred to. But she will not be able to appreciate that 'chaachi' denotes more than your father's brother's wife. 'Chaachi' carries a particular status for every member of the family. For example, the eldest 'chaachi' is the wife of the oldest son in the household, and is afforded the privilege of being the senior woman of that generation. There is quite simply no equivalent term in English for this. English culture does not distinguish relationships in this way as family structures are organised differently. The meaning of 'chaachi' is therefore lost.

Counsellors may not be able to speak Hindi, but at least they should be aware of some of the more significant values that the language connotes. The client loses all this meaning when working in English.

In another language from the Indian subcontinent, Bengali, there is no gender usage either for common nouns or pronouns. Therefore when Bengali-speaking people use English, they are unaccustomed to words such as 'she' or 'he', and may use them interchangeably. This is not to be confused with a lack of fluency in English, or as a sign of intellectual impairment !

How, then, can you as counsellors acquaint yourselves with so many nuances in other languages? As we pointed out in Chapters 2 and 3, cultural knowledge comes in many forms. Counsellors need to use their personal and institutional resources to the full in order to learn about their clients' language and culture. Specifically, we have found that reading the translated literature of a culture, from religious classics to popular novels, seeing films that depict that culture, talking to people sensitively about their culture and travelling to different countries will all help you to understand and communicate more effectively.

THE USE OF INTERPRETERS

Communication skills involve knowing how and when to use interpreters with your client from another culture. 'The right to be understood' (Shackman, 1984) is the title of a health manual about community interpreters and their use in hospitals, in social services, with the police and in law courts. This section will look at how we can use interpreters, and how they can assist the many different kinds of communication in transcultural counselling. The implication that all clients have a *right* to be understood is a radical one. Even recently, we have heard the view expressed by mental health professionals that 'foreigners' who come to the UK should learn to speak English if they wish to be able to use health and counselling services. Further, it is argued that it is in the client's own interest to do so as part of the adaptation and adjustment required of arriving in a new culture. Ethnocentric viewpoints like this are not rare. Being understood is not always seen to be a right; in some cases it has to be fought for.

If clients do not speak the majority language fluently, how do counsellors communicate with them? Counsellors often use unofficial interpreters on an ad hoc basis, for example, relatives, especially children, neighbours and strangers. Shackman (1984) lists some very real dangers in using these individuals. These include:

- inaccurate translation by unofficial interpreters;
- bias and distortion introduced by these interpreters;
- lack of confidentiality for the client;
- unofficial interpreters not understanding their role in the counselling process;
- unofficial interpreters not explaining cultural differences between the counsellor and the client;
- personal unsuitability of these interpreters in the counselling process;
- exploitation of client by unofficial interpreters;
- unofficial interpreters' overidentification with counsellor's agency, leading to bias.

The use of clients' children as interpreters in counselling may still be acceptable to some counsellors but is a practice we reject. Much interpreting deals with sensitive and difficult areas, and this places an intolerable burden both on the child and the client.

After the birth of her baby, *Mathilde* sought help from a number of agencies which had no French-speaking members of staff. Mathilde's husband accompanied her on these occasions, and the doctors and social workers who saw her asked her husband if he would interpret for them. In doing so, they had an immediate answer to a practical problem, but one that was not in the best interests of the client. It meant that Mathilde's marital problems were even less likely to be discussed, and consequently the interviews centred on her physical and emotional difficulties arising from the birth. This is not to say that spouses can never be used as interpreters: only that there are risks and limitations in such a practice, with which counsellors should acquaint themselves.

There may be occasions when a counsellor has no choice but to use an interpreter. This is not always an ideal situation but Shackman (1984) has provided a useful checklist of practical things for counsellors to do:

- check that both interpreter and client do in fact speak the same language/dialect;
- discuss beforehand with the interpreter both the content of the interview and the way in which you will both be working;
- encourage the interpreter to interrupt and intervene during the interview when necessary;
- use straightforward language;
- actively listen to both interpreter and client, including observing their body language and maintaining eye contact with both;
- allow extra time for the interview;
- check constantly your client's understanding of what has just been said;
- end the interview by asking if your client wants to raise questions or points;
- have a post-interview discussion with your interpreter about communication during the interview.

We would add the need to check out any specialist terms that might be used, and if there is linguistic equivalence for them in your client's language. If the above checklist is not used, communication can go badly wrong. For example, Shackman (1984: 34) quotes the following example:

Psychiatrist: What kind of moods have you been in recently?
Interpreter: How have you been feeling?
Patient: No, I don't have any more pain, my stomach is fine now and I can eat much better since I take the medication.
Interpreter: He says he feels fine now, no problem.

In this example, the interpreter misunderstood the use of the word 'moods' and may not have felt comfortable about asking the psychiatrist what the term meant. Furthermore, the psychiatrist did not explain to the interpreter the importance of reporting verbatim what the client says, even if the interpreter finds it silly or embarrassing.

In general, Shackman reminds us to be aware of the pressures on the interpreter. As counsellor, you are seen both by the interpreter and client as being powerful. Above all, the responsibility for the interview is yours; you will need to be alert throughout counselling and show great patience for what can be both a tedious and complex process. Henley (1979) also mentions the importance of the interpreter being acceptable to and trusted by the client. In addition, she stresses the importance of having continuity of interpreter across sessions.

Non-racist Language

Throughout this chapter, we have referred to communication very much as a skill that both parties in counselling have to acquire before a common language can be used across cultures. Counsellors' speech also reflects the attitudes and beliefs they hold about other cultures that set a particular tone to the counselling process. The counsellor's choice of language sends messages continuously to the client about the counsellor's values. Language is more than 'getting your credentials right'; it pervades the entire counselling process and will betray you if you do not genuinely respect your client's culture.

Even more than this, your thinking affects your language outside the counselling relationship. When you speak to your colleagues about your clients, you will need to reflect on which words you employ when describing people from a culture different from your own, and what you reflect about yourself when you do so.

Words change their meaning and connotation over time. Effective counsellors are aware of changes in terminology and why they have come about. For example, it is not so very long ago that people with learning disabilities were called 'idiots' and 'cretins'. When these words became used as terms of abuse, other terms such as 'mental retardates' or the 'mentally handicapped' were employed. Each new definition tries to achieve a more accurate definition of the person it describes without prejudice. Similarly, in cultural terms, words change in their connotation. For example, the words 'negro' and 'coloured' featured in general and academic use until the late 1960s. In the wake of the civil rights movement, and the work of Martin Luther King, these terms became increasingly unacceptable to black people, and fell out of use.

Counsellors need to acquaint themselves with how their transcultural clients refer to themselves and their own communities. For example, terms like 'Asian' are not only imprecise, but can give offence. Other terms such as 'immigrant', 'indigenous', 'alien', 'native', 'foreigner', 'ethnic minority', may all seem to the white counsellor as innocuous, but may have strong emotional connotations for black people. In historical terms, these words have been used in a derogatory and discriminatory way. Take the trouble to find out.

Once *Clifford* had established himself with his counsellor, he was able to vent some of the frustrations he had experienced during his life in the UK. This not only gave his counsellor a useful context in which to assess his present difficulties, but also provided her with guidelines about her own communication with him. For example, Clifford had arrived in the UK at the time of Nigerian independence. Although he is proud of his nationality, Clifford also sees Nigeria as part of the British Commonwealth and identifies with many British cultural traditions and values. He does not usually describe himself as 'African', although others have done so. Various attempts by more politicised friends to help him face British racism have made him feel confused. After years of denying racism, he is now beginning to acknowledge its impact on his own life.

His counsellor carefully investigates those cultural norms that are most comfortable and appropriate to Clifford. He is happy to think of himself and his family as British, and does not use the term 'black'. He calls himself Nigerian when he is referring to his cultural and racial origins, and indeed his only black friends are Nigerian. Clifford's right to be understood includes being able to be seen as both British *and* Nigerian by his counsellor.

In conclusion, we have seen that the client's right to be understood makes many demands of the transcultural counsellor. It is only when a common language has been established that the full work of counselling can take place. In our next chapter, we shall examine the counselling relationship itself, once counsellor and client have got started and established the client's right to be understood. In particular we shall look at the main assumptions about Western counselling practices and beliefs and how they are likely to impinge on both clients and counsellors whose backgrounds are different. We shall then highlight how these practices and beliefs affect the counselling relationship.

6

THE THERAPEUTIC RELATIONSHIP

Overview

In this chapter we shall examine how the major cultural assumptions within Western counselling models affect transcultural relationships in counselling. We shall look at specific issues of transference, power, countertransference, self-disclosure, trustworthiness and betrayal, and relate them to our four clients.

In the last two chapters, we spoke about fostering better communication with our clients across cultures. We also referred to the establishment of credentials at the start of the relationship, and the promotion of trust. These therapeutic tasks are not one-off events: rather they are the initiation of processes that will sustain the relationship. Further, because they are subject to change, they require continuous feedback and adjustment.

We have made suggestions to counsellors about how to prepare themselves for transcultural counselling. We have also looked at the conditions within which both parties have to work. This chapter will focus on the relationship between counsellor and client and how this is affected by the cultural values of Western-style counselling. These issues are inextricably linked; for example, feelings of betrayal in the relationship are manifested in the form of transference. Similarly, counsellors may establish trustworthiness in a transcultural setting through self-disclosure.

CULTURAL COMPONENTS OF THE
COUNSELLING RELATIONSHIP

This book is one of a series about different types of counselling in action, but it differs from the rest in one important respect. All but one of the titles *(Feminist Counselling in Action,* Chaplin, 1999, second edition) implicitly incorporate white Western cultural values in their approach. Katz (1985) makes the observation that Western therapies can be divided into three schools of thought: psychodynamic, existential-humanistic and behaviouristic. Further, Katz (1985: 619) asserts:

> approaches to counselling such as rational-emotive therapy, gestalt therapy, reality therapy, transactional analysis and assertiveness training are theoretically rooted in the three primary schools of thought and were developed by White practitioners enmeshed in *Western cultural values* [emphasis added]. The applicability of these theories to multicultural populations and women is questionable.

From our own working experience, we have found that our psychological training has not always provided an adequate means of dealing with cultural differences. It is these very differences that will form a barrier within the therapeutic relationship with transcultural clients. For instance, a Trinidadian client suffering from depression was referred to one of us at an earlier stage of her professional life. The client's son was afflicted with sickle-cell anaemia. At the beginning of the counselling relationship, the client exploded with rage at her white counsellor. She correctly observed that her counsellor was unlikely ever to be in the same position as her because of her race. The counsellor, inexperienced at the time, was overwhelmed by this anger and panicked; she allowed herself to remain helpless in this relationship. She could only resolve the situation by referring her client to a Caribbean community group for further help.

A more culturally skilled counsellor would not have allowed so wide a gulf to have developed in the relationship. She could have responded instead by, first, accepting her client's anger and the factual differences between them. She would then have helped her to talk through the implications of her being black, female, a single parent of a very sick child, poor and unemployed, within the context of a white, racist environment. The counsellor would recognise that she was identified as part of that environment, as well as part of the means of dealing with it.

It was this kind of experience that directed our own growth and development in counselling relationships. The burgeoning literature on the subject of transcultural counselling (Pedersen, 1985; Triandis, 1980; Sue, 1981) provides encouragement in what remains a marginalised area. We feel, however, that it is for counsellors themselves to reflect upon their own practices in therapeutic relationships. They can change their monocultural position by examining the cultural components of Western-style counselling.

In Chapter 4 we pointed out that certain characteristics in Western counselling have a strong cultural bias. As far as the therapeutic relationship is concerned, we want to examine these components, as listed by Katz (1985), and make implications for practice.

The Importance of the Individual in the Relationship

Western counselling nurtures self-centredness, self-exploration, self-disclosure and self-determination. These, in turn, create an intensity and exclusivity in the relationship which may be alien for a client from another culture. The counsellor may not take sufficient account in the relationship of the client's perception of self in relation to family, community and culture.

To be effective, the counsellor deals with the client as being an integral part of a community that consists of many significant people. In practice this means that the counsellor does not have a relationship with the client alone; members of the client's family or community may be invited to participate in the counselling sessions.

Counsellors' Status and Power

White counsellors present themselves as experts with formal credentials as well as an ethnocentric view that their mode of counselling is best. Their clients, whether they are of the same culture or not, come to share this view of counsellors as very powerful people. Furthermore, even when white counsellors are demonstrably ineffective with clients from other cultures, clients continue to believe in the counsellors' expertise.

One outcome of this myth of counsellor omnipotence is that ethnic clients come to blame themselves for failures within the relationship. To have a more effective relationship in practice, counsellors empower their clients by valuing and using their cultural knowledge. The counsellor takes the time to find out from clients those parts of their culture that are particularly significant to the therapeutic relationship. This cannot be done unless counsellors have already done some preparatory work on their clients' culture before the counselling sessions begin.

Verbal Communication

As we pointed out in chapter 5, clients have traditionally taken on the considerable burden of making themselves understood in counselling. Explicit verbal disclosures are required in the relationship, and the client from another culture has no choice but to try to conform with these difficult and unfamiliar practices. As we pointed out in the last chapter, clients who are *not* verbally fluent in counsellors' language experience greater barriers in the therapeutic relationship.

Counsellors who value the talking therapies can develop other ways in which both they and their clients can express themselves in the relationship. d'Ardenne (1986a, 1988), for example, explains the advantages of behavioural techniques over talk therapies when clients cannot use verbal communication for cultural reasons. In practice, the relationship becomes task-orientated rather than insight-orientated. Just as importantly, counsellors learn the type of non-verbal communication techniques in the relationship that we discussed in the last chapter. These include eye contact, gestures and facial expression.

Goals

Therapeutic goals of Western counselling may be unfamiliar and inappropriate ideas for clients from another culture. Helping clients achieve insight, self-awareness and personal growth may be the counsellor's goals. On the other hand, the client may want solutions to practical problems without any reference to internal change. We shall return to this theme in the next chapter which will focus on change and growth.

The counselling relationship will contain shared and appropriate goals if it is to be effective. In practice this means that the counsellor will find out from the client what are the latter's desired goals. The counsellor then explains the way counselling works and both parties negotiate a common purpose.

The Use of the Scientific Method

Western counsellors consider themselves to be objective and neutral, and to use rational and logical means of assessing, diagnosing and treating problems. A client from another culture may be seeking to form an alliance with the counsellor in the relationship. How do you retain objectivity and neutrality under these circumstances?

Culturally sensitised counsellors are able to maintain an objective stance while still supporting and accepting their clients. In practice this means that counsellors explain they cannot become personally involved with their clients. Counsellors can anticipate this issue when getting started in counselling and continue to remind their clients of it throughout the relationship.

Strict Time Boundaries

It is common for counselling sessions to run for fifty or sixty minutes, after which the encounter is ended. Clients who volunteer new or significant material at the end of their session may be testing the time boundaries within the relationship. On the other hand, they may simply be culturally unaccustomed to placing such emphasis on punctuality, and may see their counsellor as callous and rejecting if strict time limits are imposed.

In a transcultural setting, counsellors will explain what time-keeping means in counselling. They will also explore with their clients their views about time, and come to an arrangement with them that is mutually acceptable and convenient. We know of counsellors who are able to work with different cultural groups on an informal, drop-in basis, which is ideal for certain clients, but it is not without its complications. What does matter is that time-keeping gets discussed and a shared agreement concerning time boundaries is reached.

Aesthetics

Counsellors are more likely to have a successful relationship with clients who fit Katz's (1985) reference to the YAVIS client: Young, Attractive, Verbal, Intelligent and Successful. In comparison, clients from other cultures are often seen by majority culture counsellors as less attractive, less verbal, unintelligent and less successful.

The implications for practice are that counsellors should remind themselves of the danger of responding to these superficial characteristics of their clients. They can monitor the effect of their judgements about the attractiveness of their culturally different clients, and adjust their behaviour accordingly.

Historicity

In addition to Katz's list (1985), there are some additional cultural components of counselling that affect the therapeutic relationship. One of these is the great emphasis on historicity in many Western approaches to counselling. Present-day problems are seen in the context of the individual's life history and are determined by it. This approach may be a very unusual one for clients from other cultures, who see their difficulties in terms of the present. They may even feel that their counsellor is wasting valuable time in the relationship by focusing on past events.

In practice, transcultural counsellors explain their reasons for history taking, but may also have to take fewer details to accommodate their clients' viewpoint. As counsellors gain the trust of their clients in the therapeutic relationship they will be more able to return to and explore historical themes.

Non-directedness

Finally, one theme of Western counselling relationships is non-directedness. Rogers (1951: 292) asserts that 'one of the cardinal principles in client-centred therapy is that the individual must be helped to work out his own value system, with a minimal imposition of the value system of the therapist'. He points out that the counsellor's value system is itself the expression of a cultural norm. In transcultural counselling, the client may seek directives from the counsellor, and may not be able to respond to a non-directive approach. The client may even perceive the counsellor as unskilled if direct advice is not given.

In practice, counsellors will again adjust their own therapeutic style to establish an effective working relationship. This may involve their adopting a more authoritative and prescriptive stance with their clients. Triseliotis (1986) suggests that some clients from other cultures find counselling useful only if it is active, open and explicit, with specific suggestions and advice. He argues, for example, that there are black clients who go to church for reflection and inner understanding; they see their minister rather than their counsellor as helping them in that way. Similarly, clients from Asian cultures may not respond well to a reflective approach which focuses on feelings. Triseliotis (1986: 213) observes that clients from the Indian subcontinent and China 'prefer a logical, rational, structured counselling approach'. Sue and Sue (1990) believe that unstructured counselling may generate so much anxiety in the relationship as to interfere actively in therapy with culturally different clients.

In our case examples, *Rahima* repeatedly asks her counsellor for guidance about how to cope with her difficulties. It is common practice in her culture to seek specific advice from her family. Since her brother has died, she has no-one to turn to, and she therefore has to use the counsellor to give expert opinions. Her counsellor has been trained to use *non-directive* techniques, and responds initially by deflecting some of these demands. As the relationship progresses, however, the counsellor accommodates to her client's needs. When Rahima asks how she can overcome her social isolation, her counsellor makes one or two concrete suggestions for Rahima to choose from. These include inviting her next-door neighbour to her house, and re-establishing contact with some of her legal colleagues.

A related cultural component affecting the relationship between Rahima and her counsellor is that of verbal communication. After a number of counselling sessions, Rahima asks her counsellor for practical suggestions instead of just talking through her difficulties. The counsellor recognises that this is a cultural difference and uses the previous suggestions as a tangible means of testing the ideas that have been worked out during counselling.

TRANSFERENCE

'Transference' is a Western concept in therapeutic relationships, but has different meanings in different settings. In traditional psychodynamic thinking, the term 'transference' refers to '. . . the repetition by the client of old child-like patterns of relating to significant people, such as parents, but now seen in relation to the counsellor' (Jacobs, 1988:12). He argues that there are transference phenomena in all human relationships, and that counsellors can use transference to show how these feelings influence the counselling relationship.

Rogers (1951) uses the word 'transference' in counselling in a rather different way. He makes the point that the transference relationship does *not* tend to develop in *client-centred* therapy. However, transference attitudes do exist in the client, and can only be resolved when the client accepts and owns those attitudes rather than placing them on the counsellor. Here again 'transference' is used in a particular way: clients have final responsibility for their own feelings.

Smith (1985b) describes how the establishment of a transference relationship in a transcultural setting begins with finding a common reference point, for example, similarity in cultural backgrounds. By this she means that counsellors with clients who have a comparable cultural background can begin to understand their clients' world view. She believes that one of the goals of counselling is the taking on of the 'reparenting role' to help clients strengthen their ego functions. However, if white counsellors are racist, they become rejecting, critical parents who are unable to help their clients. We find this a useful caution to counsellors about the potential damage to their relationships with clients, if they are unable to examine their own cultural and racial prejudices.

For our purposes, 'transference' may be defined as the attitudes and feelings placed by the client on to the counsellor in the therapeutic relationship. In our own experience, 'transference' has an additional dimension. Clients who have had a lifetime of cultural and racial prejudice will bring the scars of these experiences to the relationship. For the most part, counsellors are from the majority culture, and will be identified with white racist society. Thus, counsellors are seen by their clients as both part of the problem and part of the solution. Their clients have no choice about this paradox, and have to work within it.

In practical terms, culturally different clients will bring their anger, distrust and fear to counselling. Within the relationship, they will act out these feelings against the counsellor. Culturally skilled counsellors can accept their clients' internal world as well as the hostile environment in which they live. They can then help their clients to cope with these feelings and to develop their own sense of powerfulness and self-esteem.

Clifford enters the counselling relationship within the context of previous encounters with white professionals who have expressed the wish to help him with his problems. With few exceptions, the authority figures in his life in the UK have been white: his employers, his manager, his shop steward, his doctors and his social worker. All of these people would claim to have had a working relationship with Clifford, and one where he was given freedom and choice in the management of his own affairs.

During session four in counselling, Clifford's politeness and deference to his counsellor begin to change.

Clifford: I guess I'm tired of the whole business. I don't want more
    worries; I want my peace.
Counsellor: You feel you want to be left alone?

Clifford: Of course I do; I'm tired of being told how to run my life.

Counsellor: Okay. What would you like now?

Clifford: I just want to know how to get well. If you're expert, tell me what to do. If you can't make me better, what's the point in coming?

Counsellor: You seem to want me to have all the answers!

Clifford: Well you're all such clever people! (laughs) You English people – always giving advice but no *real* help when I need it.

Counsellor: You feel that I, and other English people you've seen since your stroke, aren't giving you the help you really need?

Clifford: Yes. It's been nice talking and telling you about myself. But I need more. You don't understand me. You don't know what it feels like to have people treat you differently. You're as high 'n' mighty as the others.

Counsellor: I remind you of other English people who've given you a hard time. I accept that you've had to face prejudice and racism for a long time. Let's talk about these feelings now so that I can help you better.

Clifford: Okay, but you're not going to find it easy!

Clifford's growing impatience with his white counsellor reflects a change in the relationship. For the first time, he places on his counsellor his feelings about discrimination; he has experienced prejudice both because of his colour and his disability. His counsellor is both part of the oppression he is challenging and part of the help he is seeking. Thus Clifford has reached a point in the relationship where he no longer denies his experiences, but can refer for the first time to the pain of prejudice.

As a result of this, his counsellor can now explore with Clifford the impact of this pain on his present difficulties, and is able to use the relationship to provide him with the means to change and grow.

POWER

Shillito-Clarke (1996) examines ethical issues of power in the counselling relationship. The starting point is 'an imbalance of perceived power'. She reminds us that the client is vulnerable and needs to be able to trust the counsellor. Over the last decade, counsellors have addressed the power imbalance between the therapist and client, and tried to use counselling as a process of *empowerment*. Transcultural counsellors have a special responsibility to examine the power differential in their therapeutic relationship, and to make connections with the power imbalance in wider society. Lago and Thompson (1996) have highlighted the importance of the combination of prejudice and power resulting in racism. They conclude, 'If one views things from a prejudiced perspective and has the power to act out those views, the outcome is going to be racist.' (p. 21).

Lago and Thompson (1996) describe 'a powerful elite in society' where most counsellors are white, middle class and articulate. Their clients view them as superior and the effect on the therapeutic relationship is detrimental. We have already referred to the power of counsellors in Chapter 3, particularly when they are from the majority culture, and their clients are not. Furthermore, the therapeutic relationship cannot be effective if power differences are not acknowledged and tackled.

If we look again at Clifford, we have seen that the transferring of his feelings of anger on to his counsellor helps to redress the power imbalance between them. His counsellor facilitates this by accepting the anger transferred from other white people, and helping him use that anger as a way out of his own helplessness. Clifford begins to see himself as more powerful once he is able to communicate this anger and have it accepted by his counsellor.

COUNTERTRANSFERENCE

There are differing opinions about the meaning and usefulness of 'countertransference' in the therapeutic relationship. For example, Truax and Carkhuff (1967), regard it as a lack of genuineness in the therapeutic relationship. They refer to the effect of counsellors' unconscious feelings, including irrational projections and identifications, which their clients have unwittingly aroused. In practice Truax and Carkhuff (1967) stress that counsellors must not permit countertransference feelings to jeopardise the therapeutic relationship.

On the other hand, Jacobs (1988) suggests that countertransference can be either a help or a hindrance in the relationship. If the counsellor's feelings are unacknowledged, they become a 'blind spot'. If they are realistically acknowledged, countertransference can assist counselling.

When counsellor and client are from differing cultural backgrounds, countertransference invades the therapeutic relationship in a particularly insidious way. Counsellors are unlikely to examine their own racism and cultural prejudice. As a consequence of this neglect, unacknowledged prejudice is reflected back unconsciously in the therapeutic relationship. When this occurs, the client no longer experiences unconditional positive regard, genuineness and empathic understanding in the counselling relationship, and may consequently withdraw. Worse than this, the unaware counsellor only perceives the client's withdrawal as non-compliance or resistance. This dissonance in the relationship results in both parties having their beliefs about the other's culture reinforced.

There are ways for counsellors to take control and deal with this clash of beliefs. Lorion and Parron (1985) speak about 'countering the countertransference'. By this they refer to the counsellor's stereotypes about other cultures, and negative attitudes to the outcome of treatment. They conclude from the extensive literature on this subject that there may be a *causal* link between counsellors' attitudes towards their clients and therapy outcome.

In practice, it seems that when counselling is unsuccessful across cultures, counsellors tend to blame their clients as being unable to verbalise their feelings, unwilling to postpone gratification, or refusing to co-operate with treatment. Under these circumstances, counsellors communicate in an abrupt, critical and distant manner. A therapeutic relationship under such conditions can hardly survive.

Romero (1985) reminds us that counsellors are generally more comfortable dealing with their clients either as individuals or as members of the whole human race. They are less comfortable dealing with their clients in the context of their specific culture. Transcultural countertransference is not just about attitudes to other cultures. It touches our deepest fears as counsellors about being seen as judgemental and tribal. Countertransference is a painful issue, especially when the topic of racism is involved. We believe that this in part explains the shortage of literature on the subject and the way it influences transcultural counselling relationships.

The counsellor who has a therapeutic relationship with *Fred* is not culturally close to him. This becomes apparent when he sets his goals. He begins to talk about the Bangladeshi community in his neighbourhood. He is grappling both with his anxiety in social situations, as well as his prejudices.

Fred: I don't recognise this place any more. It seems to be overrun by Pakis – oh er, sorry, I don't mean you (followed by embarrassed pause).

Counsellor: You've found a lot of changes that you don't like. Do you
find it difficult seeing an Asian counsellor?
Fred: Oh no, you're different!

In this interchange, Fred's racist remark about 'Pakis' evokes intense anger in the counsellor. She responds by challenging him with a leading question about her own ethnic status, and gets in return a closed and well-defended response. She could have phrased her question in a less threatening way, for example, 'How do you feel about seeing an Asian counsellor?', and she might have been able to explore his fears more openly. As it is, her countertransference makes her question his racist attitude. She believes that racist remarks should not go unchallenged, and may result in a redefinition of the therapeutic relationship.

SELF-DISCLOSURE

There may be occasions when individual counsellors make self-disclosures. Nelson-Jones (1988) summarises very well the advantages and disadvantages. On the positive side, self-disclosure:

- demonstrates a useful relationship skill to clients
- makes counsellors appear genuine and involved
- results in sharing experiences
- provides feedback to clients
- enables counsellors to be assertive in difficult situations

However, on the negative side, self-disclosure:

- burdens clients
- gives the impression of being weak and unstable counsellors
- dominates clients
- reveals countertransference, and may be a means of manipulating clients for counsellors' needs

Sue (1981: 61) makes the point that, '. . . to prove one is trustworthy requires, at times, self-disclosure on the part of the counsellor'. Further, he asserts (Sue, 1981: 62) that 'It places the focus on the counsellor rather than the client and makes many uncomfortable. It is likely to evoke defensiveness on the part of many counselors.' In a transcultural relationship, counsellors recognise their clients' daily battle with prejudice, and demonstrate their credibility by revealing similar personal experiences to their clients.

The counsellor who has a therapeutic relationship with *Rahima* is culturally close to her. From the start of the relationship, she feels empathy with a client who was born in the same subcontinent, and has lived through the aftermath of British imperialism. There are, of course, many differences between Rahima and her counsellor but these historical and cultural ties are deeply held and are at times unconscious. For example, Rahima begins to talk about her recent life in the UK. She attempts to draw the counsellor into her world by seeking confirmation of her experiences.

> *Rahima*: You know what really irritates me? It's when strangers come up to me in the street and ask me, 'Where are you from?' They think they're being really friendly, but they're not. How dare strangers intrude upon my private life like that!
> *Counsellor*: Yes (nodding).
> *Rahima*: Ah, you've had the same experience too!
> *Counsellor*: Yes, I have. People come up to me at work and ask me the same question.

In the above exchange, the counsellor decides to use self-disclosure to share some of Rahima's pain with her. The black counsellor is able to acknowledge a subtle manifestation of racism, and validates her client's experiences by revealing some of her own encounters with white people. She does not go into great detail, however, as she would then be in danger of burdening and dominating Rahima.

TRUSTWORTHINESS

Sue and Sue (1990) believe that counsellors' self-disclosure is an important means of achieving trustworthiness in the eyes of their clients. We have already demonstrated the usefulness of self-disclosure as a therapeutic tool, when it is employed truthfully, appropriately and economically. Mearns and Thorne (1988) remind us that the development of trust within the therapeutic relationship is an ongoing process, which deepens as the two parties increase their knowledge of each other. The counsellors' trustworthiness enables clients to take risks, and makes the relationship more profound.

Sue (1981: 60) also refers to trustworthiness as encompassing 'sincerity, openness, honesty and perceived lack of motivation for personal gain'. In monocultural counselling, there is often an assumption made by both parties that counsellors are trustworthy; in transcultural counselling, the relationship can be more complicated. Clients from different cultures who have suffered prejudice and lack of economic and educational opportunities find the world to be an untrustworthy place. In the therapeutic relationship, counsellors from the majority culture therefore have to attain trustworthiness in the eyes of their clients to counteract this effect.

Mathilde's counsellor knows very early on in the therapeutic relationship that her client has been so isolated in the UK that it takes her a long time to seek help. She knows too that the discrepancy between what Mathilde expected from her confinement and what she subsequently experienced increases her sense of helplessness in what has proven to be an unreliable world. She has even begun to see her own body as somehow 'untrustworthy', that is, it hasn't performed as it is supposed to. Therefore she is being 'punished' by being compelled to have her baby in England. She feels she no longer trusts the health workers at the ante-natal clinic who reassured her throughout her pregnancy that she would be returning to France for the birth. She is critical of all who saw her and actively avoids contact with the midwives as much as possible.

Once the relationship with her counsellor is established, Mathilde begins to test her counsellor's trustworthiness:

Mathilde: What are you going to do with all those notes in my file?

Counsellor: They're here to help me. Are you worried about what's going to happen to them?

Mathilde: Of course I am! I don't want anyone at the clinic (maternity) to know that I'm not coping right now.

Counsellor: You seem to be coping very well. Tell me more about why you don't want the midwife to know you come here.

Mathilde: She'll think I'm a bad mother. You English are all the same. You don't know how awful it's been, having a baby with nobody really understanding me.

Counsellor: You feel that English people including me are not sympathetic to your needs?

Mathilde: No, but I don't see how you can understand me.

Counsellor: Maybe not. But I do have some knowledge about French life, and I can understand what it must be like to be in a foreign country.

In this way the counsellor addresses the challenge made by Mathilde in order to foster trustworthiness in the relationship. She resists the temptation to become defensive, and instead accepts Mathilde's mistrust. She then offers a cultural credential to consolidate the therapeutic relationship.

BETRAYAL

When both parties are outside the majority culture, clients sometimes see their counsellors as having 'sold out' to the establishment. Counsellors are seen as having *betrayed* their cultural background in the process of becoming a Western-style practitioner. The smaller the cultural distance between the two, the greater is the sense of betrayal.

Rack (1982) refers to the growing number of professionally trained individuals from different cultures who are working in mainstream medicine, social work and psychiatry. They were themselves born and brought up in two cultures, and have themselves assimilated the majority cultural code in their professional thinking. Rack argues that professionals from other cultures adopt the counsellor role, and are then seen as the agents of that majority culture.

Clients experience betrayal in two forms. First, counsellors who work for statutory institutions are identified, rightly or wrongly, with subjugation by the majority culture. A good example of this is the black probation officer who is seen by her black client as part of the white authoritarian racist legal system. Secondly, clients see counselling itself as an ethnocentric activity. We spoke earlier in this chapter about the Western cultural components implicit in counselling. Transcultural counsellors from outside the majority culture recognise those components and develop a more flexible working model, which combines the best of Western and other cultural practices. If they do not, there is always the risk that their clients will feel betrayed by them.

Counsellors in either of these situations can feel helpless and believe that they can do nothing that is acceptable to their clients. We suggest that they be open with their clients about their dilemma, and use it to form one of the therapeutic tasks in the relationship.

Rahima's counsellor has always been aware of this dilemma and now has to deal directly with it. She is the same age as her client's children, and yet is seen as an 'expert' by Rahima.

Rahima: I wish you would ask me more factual things, instead of all
this talk about feelings.

Counsellor: Would you feel more comfortable if we avoided talking
about anything that's upsetting, especially your children?

Rahima: I don't like talking about my children. They dumped me here
because they don't care about me any more. You may be Indian,
but you don't really care either – this is what you're paid to do.

Counsellor: I understand that you feel betrayed by your children and by
me. Your anger with them is affecting the way you see our
relationship. What would help ease that pain with your children?

Rahima's concerns are neither medical nor legal. Her children have
handed her over to a counsellor who, although Indian, may be seen as
part of a hostile external culture. Rahima's transference of her feelings
about her children on to her counsellor is her way of expressing her sense
of betrayal.

Rahima's counsellor tackles this by referring explicitly to that sense of
betrayal. She then reminds Rahima that she understands the value of
Rahima's family. Furthermore, the counsellor makes explicit her commitment to working with Rahima to achieve reconciliation with her children
on Rahima's terms.

In this chapter we have examined the effects of culture on the establishment of the counselling relationship, and used our clients to
demonstrate how the relationship becomes therapeutic. In our next chapter, we shall progress through the counselling process and consider how
change and growth can now occur for our clients in a transcultural setting.

7

CHANGE AND GROWTH

Overview

In this chapter we shall examine in some detail how counsellors facilitate their clients achieving therapeutic change, and in particular how the clients' cultural status in counselling provides a focus for growth. We shall also consider how counsellors help their clients evaluate change and monitor their progress throughout the tasks that are set in counselling. The differing cultural emphases on internal and external change will be looked at. Finally we shall consider how counsellors themselves change in their attitudes and practices in transcultural counselling.

Change and growth have occurred since the very first encounter between counsellors and clients, as we have demonstrated in earlier chapters. So far the focus has been on preparation and interpersonal processes. Transcultural work is about breaking down barriers that exist at the start of counselling, whatever the counsellors' training and background. It is only when these barriers are overcome that counsellors can extend their horizons, and help their clients achieve change within their cultural context.

The emphasis now shifts to intrapersonal events. Our four clients have a well-established transcultural relationship with their counsellors who will now help them to consolidate their therapeutic gains. They do this by jointly deciding goals with their clients, and then working out the necessary therapeutic tasks to attain those goals. Clients share their progress continuously with their counsellors, who provide appropriate feedback and encouragement at each stage of change, and a chance to reassess their clients' needs. When all this has been done, both parties are able to complete the counselling process.

INDIVIDUAL CHANGES

Clifford is able to establish his therapeutic goals with his counsellor within his first five sessions, and then work out the tasks that will be required for him to be able to reach them. Through the therapeutic relationship, his counsellor has facilitated the process by which he recognises his anger about white people in power over him, as we demonstrated in the last chapter. One of the consequences of this is that Clifford now wants to assert himself more effectively with white authority figures. In addition, he and his counsellor work out the following goals with him:

- increasing control over his life;
- gaining greater confidence and skill in speaking to strangers;
- having an active say in his rehabilitation programme;
- improving his sexual functioning with his wife.

What are Clifford's tasks? In his therapeutic relationship, Clifford begins to learn that he has repressed a great deal of his anger by denial and by avoiding occasions when he has needed to express it. This has in turn disabled him further, as he increasingly removes himself from mainstream life and contact with his own family and neighbours.

Clifford's counsellor explores various means of dealing with his difficulties. She discusses with him ways of asserting his needs without losing his temper, and uses herself as a role model to practise situations where he has previously got angry or withdrawn. Gradually, he becomes more effective at communicating his wishes, for example, through being polite and persistent.

He also discovers that he will need to face certain risks if he is to test these strategies. His counsellor accepts his speech difficulty within their relationship, which leads to his revealing his fears of being ridiculed by strangers. He realises that he avoids talking with any new people for this reason. His counsellor points out that this is the way in which he deprives himself of an important means of developing his communication skills. The counsellor helps him to see that he will have to deal with this fear in a more positive way.

Similarly, Clifford's counsellor encourages him to see the importance of talking to rehabilitation staff about his own wishes, rather than dismissing their help as being inappropriate. He begins to assume more responsibility for his health and resettlement, and decides to work out with the staff a jointly agreed programme. As Clifford's ability to change his relationship with the outer world begins to increase, so does his motivation to tackle the problem of his erectile failure. His counsellor establishes that he has not shared this problem with his wife, and that he has seen the dysfunction as his and his alone. When she invites his wife to one of the counselling sessions to give her side of the story, Clifford is able to share the problem more easily, and agrees to undertake some conjoint therapy.

His goal is to improve their communication and sexual technique, even if the central sexual difficulty is not solved. The counsellor offers Clifford and his wife a fixed number of sessions of sexual counselling. Here, the counsellor places emphasis on joint responsibility for change in a carefully graded programme, where they choose their goals together in a systematic and practical way. Clifford views this very positively, as it provides him with a chance of sharing achievement with his wife in a neglected part of their intimate life together.

In conclusion, it appears that Clifford's growth in counselling starts when his counsellor enables him to locate his anger against racism correctly. Once this has been done, he can achieve a sense of powerfulness through exploring other ways of functioning in a safe relationship with a white counsellor.

Mathilde and her counsellor also have a full and pressing agenda. We have pointed out how Mathilde came into counselling wanting to deal with practical issues concerning childcare, but took the risk of mentioning her relationship with her husband as early as the first session. The counsellor recognises that transcultural difficulties will need to be addressed and resolved first. It is only when Mathilde feels 'safer' in her new culture that her counsellor will offer her a chance to look at her marriage in more depth. The counsellor does not set goals as formally as with Clifford, but she does nevertheless identify four areas of growth and change with Mathilde:

- improving care for her baby;
- achieving a sense of perspective and self-confidence outside her own culture;
- expressing emotional needs in a healthy, that is non-medicalised, way;
- increasing her trust in her husband.

Mathilde's counsellor quickly grasps how much her client's self-esteem would be improved if she could 'get on top' of her childcare anxieties. As we pointed out in the last chapter, Mathilde's world has so far proved to be unreliable; even her body has 'let her down'. She is obliged to have her baby away from home without the advice she expected from those she trusted. Her fears of neglecting her baby led her to bottle-feed when she wanted to breast-feed, and she constantly seeks reassurance about her maternal status instead of trusting her own judgement.

The counsellor helps Mathilde share her sense of dislocation and helplessness. Gradually Mathilde feels accepted by her counsellor and starts to share her ideas more constructively instead of asking for advice. On one occasion, Mathilde brings her baby with her to counselling, and her counsellor encourages her to hold him, rock him, talk to him and tell him how much she loves him and cares for him. The counsellor thus gives her client permission to be a mother in a spontaneous and personal way.

In a few weeks Mathilde plucks up courage to ask the health visitor who comes to her home for contacts with mother and baby groups. Although her English is limited, Mathilde recognises the value of self-help activities and resolves to join a local weekly gathering for company and support.

Mathilde is also changing her ideas about her transcultural experiences. Her counsellor represents a stepping stone between her own culture and that in which she now lives. The counsellor affects Mathilde's views about herself as a 'foreigner'. The counsellor offers both French and English language counselling, and Mathilde continues to speak mainly French with her. But as her sense of acceptance in counselling grows, Mathilde starts to seek more English language contacts in her neighbourhood and to make a serious effort to communicate with those around her. She still feels 'stupid' when she makes errors or forgets words, but perseveres, listens to English radio and television, and registers for a course in pottery at a local evening class. She deliberately avoids a language class as she wants to meet English people, and have a non-language focus for her activity.

Mathilde has spent a lot of her time in the UK as somebody's patient. Her doctor has diagnosed her as depressed, and she very quickly adopts a 'sick' role. The counsellor explores other possibilities with Mathilde, who discovers that she can use her new community contacts to find ways of saying what she wants in a direct and appropriate fashion, instead of being a needy person with a mental health problem.

This is not to say that Mathilde does not sometimes feel depressed or helpless; rather that she now has a wider repertoire of ways of responding to those feelings, and sharing them with others. For example:

Mathilde: I wish I was up to coping with a dinner party for my husband's colleagues.

Counsellor: What stops you?

Mathilde: Well, I would only get anxious and let him down at the time; I'm so useless on big occasions. I'd get panicky if the baby didn't settle, and then I'd start to cry and get depressed again.

Counsellor: You want to be the perfect hostess, and if you're not, then you're no good for anyone.

Mathilde: Why am I like that? Some Englishwomen I've met look after each other's babies for an evening, and then entertain without fuss. They don't seem to think there's anything strange about that. None of my friends or family would do such a thing in France. I've never let the baby stay with anyone else.

Counsellor: Maybe you'd like to, but don't dare, because you think people will see you as not coping. But if you did a swop with one of the women in your groups who already babysits, you'd be doing her a favour too.

Mathilde: I'll think about it.

Mathilde's husband, John, is supportive of her attempts at change and babysits when she is out of the house. He wants to help in any practical way he can. He is, however, only partially aware of Mathilde's unresolved struggle with him about power and control, which we have already mentioned in an earlier chapter. He has come to see Mathilde as a sick woman, who needs lots of care and attention.

As the counsellor highlights areas where Mathilde can take on more responsibilities for herself, Mathilde becomes more confident, and stops blaming John and their move to the UK for her own sense of powerlessness. In turn, John no longer needs to be the 'strong' partner who has to care for, and protect, Mathilde from a hostile culture. He is then able to express need and weakness more openly to her, and provide her with an opportunity to give and share. The counsellor offers Mathilde a safe place to examine this changing balance in the marriage, and to consider her relationship with John as an equal partnership based on mutual trust and dependence.

In summary, Mathilde will continue to make many other changes in her new culture. Her counsellor has offered a relationship that values her unconditionally. Mathilde is now in a stronger position to assume responsibility for those changes and to handle loss and disappointment without becoming clinically depressed.

Fred's counsellor has already helped him to tackle some of his own concerns about working with women and especially with an Asian woman by the time his counselling relationship is established. The process of change and growth begins as soon as he meets his counsellor. We have already referred to the psychological strategies Fred uses to co-operate with his counsellor; namely that he thinks of her as a 'professional' relative of his doctor.

Gradually, the counsellor's acceptance of Fred enables him to focus on her as a professional instead of 'yet another Asian'. He starts counselling in an aloof and untrusting way, but then becomes increasingly accepting of his counsellor. He sets goals with her cautiously, starting with his outer world, and ending with his more intimate relations. His goals may be summarised as:

- freeing himself from social anxieties;
- finding himself a job;
- improving communication and assertiveness with his wife;
- interacting with his children on an adult-to-adult basis.

The counsellor gets Fred to look at his anxiety when in the company of others. He recognises that some of it is displaced hostility towards people in his neighbourhood who have changed it beyond recognition. We have already referred to 'yuppies' who have caused the cost of housing to increase, and to the Bangladeshi members of the community whom Fred sees as taking all the local jobs. His counsellor skilfully takes Fred through these painful areas to a point where he is able to understand that his anger stems from helplessness.

He reminisces about the old East End and his life on the docks His counsellor knows little about this, and explores his past with him. She does this partly to provide Fred and herself with clues for change, and partly to increase Fred's confidence in his past achievements. One of Fred's hobbies was dog breeding, an activity that brought him into contact with a wide variety of people and made him some extra money. He gave this up when he moved to his present flat, though he reports that one of his boys has also started dog breeding. Fred has a wide knowledge about dogs, and his counsellor provides him with a relationship where he can talk about this important feature of East London culture with great interest and pride.

In doing so, he rediscovers some of his self-respect and resolves to look up some of his old dog-loving drinking friends at the pub. He knows that this remains an important means of feeling more at ease with others. More than this, dog breeding will provide Fred with access to the world of work. He has a wide informal network of friends, with whom he has lost contact since his illness, and who would be able to find him some part-time activity.

Once the counsellor has discussed Fred's outer world and activities, she ventures into the more fraught area of his relationship with his wife, Anne. The marriage is complicated by many issues. Anne in part represents the middle-class aspirations he has come to despise in those around him. All this is made worse by the fact that she is in a well-paid job, which makes him feel inferior and worth less than her.

The counsellor decides to invite Anne to attend two sessions to look more at these issues. Anne appears sympathetic to Fred, but says she is not willing to change her lifestyle, nor to comply with a more traditional marital role. She recognises that Fred's self-confidence can be enhanced by his finding work for himself, and through both of them communicating more effectively and demonstrating more affection to each other. Fred and Anne agree to some conjoint marital therapy. The counsellor recommends another agency because she already has a therapeutic alliance with Fred alone. Anne accepts that she does have some responsibility for change too, but wants to share that responsibility with her husband, rather than change on her own.

Fred's counsellor knows that once the power issues between husband and wife have been examined, it will be easier to help him look at his relationship with his sons, with whom he has always had difficulties. He has coped with their dissent against him by becoming increasingly authoritarian, and occasionally violent, as was his father to him. As long as the boys were young, and living at home, this 'worked'.

Now that Fred's sons have lives of their own, he feels unable to control them, and has never considered another kind of relationship with them. This is in marked contrast to Anne, and has proved to be a source of arguments within the family. Fred's counsellor is able to make the connections between his working more closely with Anne, and approaching his sons on an adult basis. As his self-respect returns, he begins to talk about activities he can share and enjoy with his sons, including dog breeding. Little by little, he adopts a more open, less defensive stance with them when they come to the house, and is able to 'be himself' instead of playing the role of 'big daddy'.

Overall, Fred is given a chance to find himself by returning to skills and activities in his past and developing them for the future, rather than berating what is new and changing around him. The fact that his counsellor is black enables him to break one stereotype about Asian people being poor and ignorant. The fact that he can work with a woman breaks another stereotype about his always being more comfortable with men. These internal changes enable Fred to see that there are others he can make that affect the world outside himself too.

Rahima was referred to counselling somewhat against her will by her son, Farooq. Her counsellor is hardly surprised, therefore, that her client wants something in her relationship with him to change. As with Fred, the counsellor examines Rahima's attempts to be an authoritarian parent, and why she is no longer able to achieve what she wants. Rahima is caught between the old life and the new, and the counsellor encourages her to articulate her sense of cultural displacement Only then can the counsellor get Rahima to decide on counselling goals that will provide her with directions for the future. Rahima's goals are:

• forming a harmonious relationship with her children;
• being able to rely on them in times of illness and need;
• re-establishing social contact with friends and former colleagues;
• deciding where to spend the rest of her life.

The counsellor places responsibility for change firmly in Rahima's court, and asks her what changes she is willing to undertake to achieve conciliation with her children. The counsellor explicitly acknowledges the importance of Rahima's traditional role as head of the family. But she then demonstrates how it could be more effective if Rahima were able to recognise her children's needs and to meet them on a reciprocal basis. One of the ways she does this is by discussing Rahima's late brother, and the influence he had on the family.

> *Counsellor*: How did your children get on with your brother?
> *Rahima*: Oh, they loved him. He was always kind and considerate to them. He had time for each of them.
> *Counsellor*: I wonder what sort of things he did to win such a special place in the family?
> *Rahima:* Well, he never shouted, and he listened very carefully. I never felt I was struggling against him, as I do with my children.
> *Counsellor*: Now that sounds important. Can you compare his handling of the family with your own?

Rahima: (becoming tearful) I've made such a mess of it all.
Counsellor: It's hard, isn't it, bringing up your children on your own in
another culture.

Gradually, Rahima comes to see that her sternness is much more related
to her own needs than to those of her children. Rahima and her counsellor work out some practical tasks together. One of these is breaking the
habit of waiting for her children to telephone her every day. She decides
that she will telephone them instead, and practises what she will say to
them with her counsellor.

This simple initiative becomes a significant breakthrough for her. By
calling her children, she is no longer the passive, 'wronged' party, and is
able to express herself in a more constructive way. For their part, her children start to listen to her more attentively and develop a healthier and
more open relationship with her. Rahima also listens more attentively.
She has always had the most stormy relationship with her eldest son,
Farooq. The counsellor helps Rahima work out how she is going to
resolve the situation with him. For the first time, Rahima plans to give him
the opportunity to talk on his terms, rather than hers.

At the following session, Rahima tells the counsellor how she has taken
Farooq out to dinner. There, he talked about the difficulties he has faced
in coming to the UK. He spoke about the culture shock and racism he suffered when he arrived as a seven-year-old from Bengal. He said that these
experiences have never left him, and that they have profoundly influenced
his view of life in the UK. He talked about being the oldest son, and how
he has had to shoulder greater responsibility for the family. He felt that
this has never been acknowledged. Without his father, he has had to support his mother, and was not free to express his own sense of loss and
alienation in a culture he did not choose to live in.

Rahima tells her counsellor how pleased she is to have had this conver-
sation with Farooq. Her counsellor responds by being supportive, but
recognises that this account is a censored one. She then asks Rahima if
there had been any difficult moments during the meal. She is able to share
with the counsellor Farooq's anger, some of which was directed at her.
The counsellor helps her to accept that this is only the start of reconciliation.

Rahima also reveals her long-held fears about becoming disabled and
dependent as she gets older. She believes that she will be abandoned to an
old folks' home, as she views her children as having adopted Western-style
values about care of the elderly. Rahima's counsellor encourages her to

express these fears to her children, who are able, in turn, to reassure her that she will be a part of their family and they will care for her always. The discussion about old age leads Rahima on to the subject of whether or not she will return to her place of birth before she dies. She has in the past frequently talked about 'going home' although she recognises that 'home', as it was for her before Indian partition, no longer exists. The counsellor is not able at this stage to help Rahima resolve the matter, but she does at least explore with her the possibility of returning.

Finally, Rahima realises that her own preoccupations within her family life have distanced her from her friends and former legal colleagues. As she takes more control of her life, she is able to initiate contact with some of these people and develop her social life again. All these changes have only just begun, and her counsellor reassures her that she will be able to continue making them step by step. Nevertheless, Rahima has reached a significant breakthrough in her difficulties, and one which will have an effect on every part of her life at present.

EVALUATION

With each of their clients, counsellors focus on the importance of evaluating changes over time. Many of the cultural barriers between counsellors and clients have been tackled in the relationship, and during therapeutic change. Evaluation, therefore, will place less emphasis on cultural issues as both parties reach a transcultural understanding.

Evaluation has the effect of showing clients that progress has been made in counselling. Clients have achieved change and growth in ways that are appropriate both within their own culture and in that of the majority culture. Evaluation also encourages clients to persevere with their therapeutic work. Evaluation can take many forms: either counsellors assess and provide direct feedback, or clients themselves monitor their own changes and discuss them with their counsellors. This is a dynamic process and provides both parties with a way of clarifying and redefining their goals.

The counsellor discusses with *Clifford* ways of measuring his progress. He decides to keep a *diary* because it is confidential and he can write it at his own pace. He notes the occasions when he talks with strangers, and how anxious he feels about it. He then brings the diary to his counselling sessions, first to provide a focus for discussion, and secondly to measure the changes that he has made. He takes this diary when he visits his speech therapist, and shows her how much he has achieved. The diary itself becomes a part of his rehabilitation programme. This simple form of self-monitoring is a more powerful motivator for Clifford than anything the counsellor might have said to him about his achievements. In every sense he 'owns' it.

Fred requires a graded approach to changing his anxiety about social-ising again. He draws a plan of gradual steps that will eventually lead to his recommencing dog breeding. He starts by subscribing to a dog breed-ers' magazine and updating his knowledge. After this and other steps, Fred discusses his progress and any difficulties he has experienced during these tasks with his counsellor.

His next step is to visit a local club where he is likely to meet his old friends, and re-establish contacts. In this way, Fred builds up his courage and is able to take on increasingly challenging tasks. If at any stage he feels overwhelmed by anxiety, his counsellor shows him how to break the task down further into more manageable steps, so that he feels in control at every stage of change. By 'reporting in' at each phase, he has the chance to register his own responses and gauge his progress throughout.

INTERNAL VERSUS EXTERNAL CHANGE

All our clients have been involved in initiating both internal and external changes in their lives. By internal changes we mean clients altering their subjective inner world, whether it be thoughts, feelings or attitudes. By external changes, we mean clients altering directly their outward world, whether it be relationships, activities or personal circumstances. These two aspects of change are intimately linked and interact with each other.

For example, as a result of *Mathilde* achieving internal change in shar-ing her sense of dislocation and alienation with her counsellor, she is enabled to take the first external step of joining a self-help mothers' group. This in turn provides her with additional feedback about herself, and increases her self-esteem and confidence. Thus she feels able to proceed to other changes.

In *Rahima's* case, when she undertakes an external change, for example telephoning her children, her internal perceptions of her family alter. She listens more effectively and begins to understand them better. This itself enables Rahima to reflect on other changes, both internal and external, that could be possible for her.

The external environment for clients from other cultures may need much greater focus than for those from the majority culture. This is because of the alienating influence of the majority culture, and its power to create a chronic sense of 'loss'. As Fernando (1986: 130) observes: 'In dealing with a depressed person one should try to identify the blows to self-esteem in recent events that arise from racism. An awareness of what happens is important because the patient has to develop strategies to safeguard self-esteem . . .'. An acknowledgement of that external reality and its contribution to depression is essential in order to help clients develop strategies for coping with it.

Smith (1985b) has devised a very useful Stress Resistant Delivery (SRD) model for counselling 'racial minorities', which is fundamentally different from traditional Western-style counselling. She outlines three basic stages of this approach as:

- counsellors need to identify the origins of clients' stress;
- counsellors need to investigate both the internal and external precipitants of stress, as well as the coping mechanisms of clients both individually and in the context of their own culture;
- counsellors must then work out a way of delivering services to their clients based on the above considerations.

The ways in which changes occur reflect the particular circumstances of the client, the level of trust achieved with the counsellor, the readiness of the client to tackle a particular difficulty and cultural expectations of change.

There are different emphases on change in every culture. Smith (1985a), for example, points out that black Americans would find it more appropriate to seek help from family members or ministers of the church in dealing with the inner self. Counsellors will be sought for specific practical advice about the outer world. In a similar vein, Triseliotis (1986: 212) concludes, '. . . because of cultural factors, some ethnic minority clients respond better to more active, more open and clear approaches, which include suggestions, as compared with the mostly reflective, rather introspective and totally permissive forms of counselling used by white counsellors.'

It is difficult to generalise more than this. If asked, clients will tell us what they want and what they expect of counselling. It is for us as counsellors to listen to the responses, and to provide clients with every opportunity to express their hopes and wishes.

FEEDBACK

We have already spoken about feedback in the process of evaluating and monitoring changes in counselling. But there is a continuous process that takes place between the two parties that allows them to assess the significance of change and growth in the relationship. Nelson-Jones (1988) calls this 'open mutual feedback'. Such a process affords both counsellor and client the chance to communicate to the other what is happening inside and outside themselves. Sensitive counsellors will recognise the importance of using feedback as an opportunity for them to improve their cultural knowledge, and thereby enhance the therapeutic effect. For example, in *Clifford's* case:

> *Clifford*: Why are you never angry with me?
> *Counsellor*: Why should I be angry with you?
> *Clifford*: Because you only smile when we start and when we go. The rest of the time you just look polite, like all my English friends, and I don't know what you're thinking. I just wish you'd shout or laugh. Then I'd feel more comfortable with you.
> *Counsellor*: You'd like me to show my feelings more? I hadn't realised that; that's very useful.

The counsellor acknowledges the feedback and will pay closer attention to her non-verbal communication in future.

In another vein, clients provide feedback about changes from inside and outside counselling. In this way, they give their counsellors a chance to see how they are testing out those changes. For example, *Rahima* has a next-door neighbour whom she has known 'over the hedge' for many years. During counselling, Rahima resolves to invite her into her home for coffee. Her neighbour comments how over the past few weeks Rahima seems to be much more active than usual. Rahima brings this to the next counselling session with some delight.

> *Rahima*: I can't imagine why I should be so pleased about what she said.
> *Counsellor*: Maybe it's good to feel you're not the only person to notice how you've changed.
> *Rahima*: That's it! I know I've changed, but my neighbour knows me so little, and even she can see the difference – so it must be real!
> *Counsellor*: Will you see her again?
> *Rahima*: Oh yes, I want to get to know her better.

CHANGES IN THE COUNSELLOR

Most of this chapter has focused on the traditional notion of therapeutic changes that take place in clients as a result of counselling. Transcultural counselling, however, gives both parties a unique chance to achieve personal growth.

In Chapter 2, we spoke about counsellors' cultural knowledge, and the ways in which it needed to be developed for transcultural counselling to be successful. This knowledge is not static and has undergone change throughout the relationship. The most important changes in counsellors may be those of perception and understanding of their clients' culture. Counsellors come face to face not only with their clients' experience of prejudice, restricted economic and social opportunities, but also the wealth of their family life, their language and traditions. From this, counsellors grow in their understanding of the additional effort and complexity involved in their clients communicating across cultures.

The counselling relationship gives counsellors an authentic opportunity to experience these barriers. For example, counsellors may find that they can never fully communicate their ideas and feelings to their clients, or that their counselling manner might be interpreted as hostile. This is precisely what clients from other cultures have to face all the time. Counsellors come to understand what this feels like and use these experiences in transcultural counselling.

Changes in attitude create changes in counsellors' practice. Counsellors themselves adjust and acculturise to their altered circumstances, just as clients have to. *Clifford's* counsellor, for example, takes his feedback about laughing seriously enough to be able to laugh with him. Transcultural counselling demands creativity and flexibility in order to be effective.

Transcultural counsellors face other challenges. After the immediacy of working with clients across cultures, counsellors will demonstrate to their colleagues the value of this approach. In a wider context, they will try to persuade professional bodies, training resources and funding agencies to change. What we have tried to show is that change and growth start within counsellors, and have very far-reaching effects.

In conclusion, we have examined the major therapeutic changes and areas of growth in our four clients. We have discussed ways in which transcultural counsellors develop appropriate strategies to facilitate that change. The ways in which those changes are registered, and the particular significance they have for the clients have also been discussed. Change is dynamic and interactional and occurs internally as well as externally, sometimes with widespread effect. In our final chapter, we shall see the completion of the therapeutic process. Suggestions will be made about how counsellors bring counselling to an end with clients across cultures, and encourage them to use all the resources that continue to be available.

8

ENDINGS

Overview

In this chapter our clients who have completed their counselling tasks will review with their counsellors the progress that has been made. We will also consider how to obtain and use feedback from clients. Skills for ending counselling will be examined, including how to manage relapse, and how to negotiate further contact. The effects of endings on counsellors themselves will be reviewed. Finally, we shall look at how clients can be directed towards alternative resources when they have ended transcultural counselling.

This is the last time we shall consider *Clifford, Fred, Mathilde* and *Rahima*, as they complete the counselling process, and continue with their lives independently. We shall look at the ways in which our four clients are prepared for the end of transcultural counselling. Some of the feelings that are expressed at the end of counselling are often associated with bereavement (Parkes, 1986), including avoidance or denial, anger, sadness and acceptance of loss. Parkes (1986) argues that loss and separation are both a threat to one's established life, as well as an opportunity for gaining mastery of it. If counsellors help their clients to face endings and loss in a *planned* way, then this change can lead to their being able to achieve control over their lives.

Separation is just as much an issue for counsellors as for clients when they have both worked at breaking down cultural barriers. This partnership brings the counsellor and client together in a particular way, and letting go of that relationship may be painful for both. Transcultural counsellors are aware of these dynamics and assume responsibility for their own sadness and worries about their clients.

TRANSCULTURAL ENDINGS

Endings entail issues around the completion of counselling; they are also about anticipating future difficulties and ensuring that clients have continuing access to help. In any counselling, clients and counsellors have different views about the time-scale for ending counselling. Similarly, there are cultural differences about the circumstances under which endings occur. This may even be the case when clients are culturally very distant from their counsellors, and where the possibility of misinterpretation is therefore all the greater. Thus, *Fred* and *Clifford* are also vulnerable to misunderstanding the purpose behind the termination of counselling. Their counsellors, therefore, will need to employ transcultural skills to prevent their sense of being dismissed from counselling.

Counsellors also have special needs as transcultural counselling reaches an end. Counsellors will sometimes experience difficulties during the counselling process. One reason for these obstacles may be that counsellors fail to recognise their own sense of helplessness with clients from other cultures. Another may be that counsellors' prejudices interfere with the ending of counselling. These reasons lead to important consequences at the end of the process.

First, counsellors may finish counselling too early and leave their clients feeling spurned. Clients from other cultures may already have experienced a sense of rejection, both in their private world and in their dealings with professionals. Counsellors should ensure that their own prejudices, or lack of sensitivity, do not lead to their terminating counselling prematurely.

Secondly, counsellors may 'hang on' to clients who have completed their tasks, making their clients over-dependent. In most transcultural settings, counsellors are members of the white, dominant cultures. By keeping their clients too long, these counsellors may, in a subtle way, reinforce a stereotype about white culture being the best and the most powerful.

Thirdly, as the final part of counselling, 'endings' may carry the most powerful memories about the whole counselling process, a phenomenon known as the 'recency effect'. The consequence of a mishandled ending in counselling is that the productive work that has been done will be discounted by both parties. It is more likely that they will remember that their relationship ended badly.

COMPLETION OF THERAPEUTIC TASKS

The completion of therapeutic tasks is dependent on the quality of the therapeutic relationship. There are individual differences in perception of whether tasks have been completed or not. Unless there has been good communication and agreement between both parties, counselling will end on a discordant note.

In addition to individual differences in the way clients perceive the completion of their tasks, there are also cultural variations. In the last chapter we spoke about those cultures that focus on external change in counselling. When individual clients have achieved external as well as internal growth, those clients may not be able to acknowledge that internal change has occurred.

Fred is a good example of this. He initially completes many of his external tasks, such as getting involved in dog breeding again and talking to his sons on a more equal basis. He talks about his external world in a more confident and positive manner, and has made plans to visit a dog-breeding exhibition in Yorkshire. This is all the more remarkable in a man who has not left London for the last eight years. His counsellor acknowledges his achievements, and then turns to his internal world.

> *Counsellor*: But you've changed in other ways, Fred. You seem to have gained so much confidence in yourself, as well as others.
> *Fred*: Do you really think so? I can't say I've really thought much about it. I thought it was more important to get back in touch with my old friends.
> *Counsellor*: And what do you think now?
> *Fred*: Maybe you've got a point!

Fred is at first surprised that his internal change 'counts', but after some deliberation, he agrees that he has been able to grow from within. His counsellor makes it clear that both kinds of change are valuable and noticeable, and does not express any preference for one kind or another.

FEEDBACK

Feedback is an essential ingredient in ending all counselling; transcultural counselling is no exception. Its relevance at the end of counselling is to enable clients to give a full account of their experiences, and for clients to reflect on changes that have occurred. Clients may have a range of topics to discuss, for example, their feelings about the relationship, or the counsellor's techniques, all of which will enable both parties to assess how successful transcultural counselling has been. For example, during feedback *Clifford* tells his counsellor:

> I'm glad I came here. I seem to have sorted out some of my
> problems. But you shouldn't cut me off as I'm telling you
> important things – how can you help me if you cut me off?
> *Counsellor*: I'm sorry you feel that way. I realise now we could have
> been more flexible with time if we'd met at the end of the day. As
> it is, you feel rejected because I always ended the sessions
> promptly.

In this example we see that the question of strict time-keeping in counselling still represents a barrier between Clifford and his counsellor. Clifford's counsellor thought it would be sufficient to discuss it when getting started. But for Clifford, the issues are much deeper than this. He sees the Western preoccupation with time as rigid and intimidating, and even feels that his counsellor rejects him at the end of each session.

The counsellor will not necessarily extend her time boundaries with all her future clients. However, she will be able to use Clifford's feedback to ensure that, in future, she checks out issues like time regularly with clients, especially when she knows that her clients hold culturally different perceptions from her.

REVIEW

Once counsellors have received feedback from their clients, they are responsible for initiating and carrying out a review of the entire counselling process. We have found that the more clients are able to participate in this process, the more likely they are to remember and consolidate the changes they have undergone. Some workers (Nelson-Jones, 1988) suggest the use of tape-recordings to help both parties review their work together.

In a transcultural setting, we find this is often inappropriate. Our clients may be suspicious of recordings, or see them as a very strange way of conducting the counselling session, even when a full explanation is given.

Client involvement may not be a sufficient means to a full review. In these circumstances, counsellors can be directive with their clients about the changes achieved. Emotional changes need special care in review, because clients from other cultures have so often had their feelings misinterpreted by people from the dominant culture.

Mathilde very much enjoys doing her review with her counsellor. She is able to refer to many changes that have taken place in her life, and is particularly aware of how new friends have seen her develop. It seems that Mathilde is very able to identify with the new mothers that she now meets, and she now places value on how English people see her.

Her counsellor points out how different her feelings towards English people have become, and she expresses some embarrassment and guilt when looking back at how she spoke about them earlier in counselling. Her counsellor explores these feelings with her.

> *Counsellor*: Why do you think your attitude towards English people has changed?
> *Mathilde*: I used to lump all English people with John – because he didn't understand me, I thought nobody here did. It's not that straightforward any more. I've met some women in the group whom I get on with. But it doesn't mean I like everybody here.
> *Counsellor*: You've learned not to generalise. Tell me more about how you've changed in your feeling towards John.
> *Mathilde*: I was blaming him for anything I couldn't cope with. I still think he could have helped me more, but I realise that I tend to get angry with others when I'm really angry with myself.

In this exchange, Mathilde realises that she has always blamed others for her difficulties, and that this happened in France long before she met John. Mathilde discovers that now she is aware of this, she can opt for greater responsibility for herself. Her counsellor responds to this by reviewing Mathilde's actual achievements in the previous weeks towards self-responsibility. She concludes that Mathilde has already started this process.

SKILLS FOR ENDING

Clients need to understand from the very beginning of the relationship that there will be an end to the counselling process. Engagement is already a preparation for disengagement and it is the responsibility of counsellors to remind their clients of this, even at the start of the counselling relationship.

Counsellors take account of the feeling of *loss* and separation that all clients will experience at the ending stage of counselling. Culturally different clients may be reminded of other losses already suffered in their transcultural status. In preparing these clients for endings, counsellors will search for echoes of loss in their clients' past, and the experiences of rejection. Counsellors will then make associations between these and help their clients find a constructive way of dealing with their losses.

Clifford is particularly sensitive to loss. He has lost many opportunities for better education and jobs because of racism. He has been given a redundancy notice at his place of work. He has been discharged from an acute medical ward with little understanding of his condition. His son has emigrated to Nigeria without consulting him; and he now faces the end of an intimate and supportive therapeutic relationship. He is able to explore the implications of this current loss with his counsellor, something which he has never previously been able to do. His counsellor helps him to make the connections between all these losses. Unlike the other losses, the end of counselling is within his control. He is able to state the terms under which it will happen, and have time to plan positively for his future.

Clifford: I guess I won't be coming in much more from now on.
Counsellor: (smiles) You feel we've done our work together?
Clifford: Yes. I haven't got all my confidence back as yet, but I do feel better than I did when I first came. So, I think it's time to end, don't you?
Counsellor: How many more times would you like to come in?
Clifford: Well, maybe two more times is enough.
Counsellor: That seems about right.

DECREASING CONTACT

One useful way of helping clients become more independent of the counselling process is to decrease the frequency of sessions. Clients need to be actively involved in preparing for this and in deciding the rate at which sessions will be reduced. If clients are not given this opportunity, there is the risk that they will seek a way of maintaining the relationship in an unhealthy manner.

Rahima sees no reason to end the counselling relationship. She has made changes in her life, but is very comfortable with her counsellor, and does not want to lose her. Earlier, they discussed dependence issues in the therapeutic relationship, and these resurface at the point of disengagement. Rahima has turned her counsellor into the 'perfect child' who is now about to abandon her. Rahima attempts to evoke guilt in her counsellor by saying:

> How can you leave me at such an important time? I still haven't worked out what to do about Abdul (her younger son).
> *Counsellor*: What do you think will happen if I'm not here?
> *Rahima*: If Abdul refuses to see me, I'll have no-one to help me sort out what to do.
> *Counsellor*: You've already learnt a great deal from your experience of dealing with Farooq.
> *Rahima*: Well (pause), I suppose so.
> *Counsellor*: You seem frightened of coping with your children on your own.
> *Rahima*: Well, what do you expect after all the problems I've had with them for so many years?
> *Counsellor*: I agree. You've had long-standing difficulties. But the difference now is that you've had a number of experiences in dealing with them in a conciliatory way.

Her counsellor takes this further and discovers that Rahima is fearful of having sole responsibility for her life. She sees this as a solitary state, and worries about her relationship with her children reverting to their previous condition. Rahima's culture emphasises reliance and mutual caring, but she finds it hard to achieve this sense of security in her own family. She therefore relies on her counsellor for unconditional support. Her counsellor reminds Rahima of the skills she has acquired in improving her relationship with her children. She asks her to reassess her resources and in particular her ability to take risks with them.

Gradually, as Rahima's counsellor feeds back to her how she has gained confidence in herself, Rahima is able to set a timetable for reducing contact with her counsellor. She is used to coming in every week and Rahima initially proposes that she come in every second week for the following month. Her counsellor suggests that she can make brief telephone contact if she should feel that she cannot cope in between.

UNFINISHED BUSINESS

While negotiating the decrease in frequency of sessions, counsellors must give their clients an opportunity to mention again any 'unfinished business'. By this we mean difficulties that have been alluded to in the therapeutic relationship, but not dealt with in any detail. Reasons for this include the limited counselling time available, the relevance of the material to the client's stated goals, and the changing agenda of the client in the counselling process. Unfinished business also refers to material that has been tackled but not resolved satisfactorily. Avoidance of difficult issues by both parties, prejudices on either side and lack of counsellor's skill may account for this. Counselling cannot be completed unless unfinished business is openly discussed. During endings, counsellors schedule enough time for discussion of this subject, as this will be their clients' final chance for counselling.

Transcultural counsellors exercise caution in distinguishing between those items that they can take up in counselling, and those which will be referred outside the counselling relationship. What we mean here is that issues concerning advocacy, liaison or the provision of material resources must be negotiated with the client, the counsellor and other agencies. These decisions have to be dealt with before ending counselling, in order to save clients from relapse.

Clifford provides us with a good example. When his counsellor raises the subject of decreasing sessions, she also asks if there is anything else that is of concern to Clifford. After some reflection, he indicates that he has grown increasingly dissatisfied with his job, since he has recommenced work at the car factory. He then goes on to ask if he could have some vocational guidance, as he feels that he is not in the right line of work. He feels unfulfilled as a car assembly worker, but was forced into this job many years ago. He had hoped to get a higher education, and tried unsuccessfully to get into college. He now sees discriminatory practices rather than his own lack of qualifications as the reason for this. Clifford's achievements in counselling encourage him to seek other changes in his life.

His counsellor reminds him that there are bound to be many knock-on effects in his life, as a result of the changes he has made, both in his rehabilitation programme and in his personal relationships. This particular concern about his job, however, is not within the remit of his present counselling. She recognises that this is an important but separate agenda that will require specialist input over an extended period of time. She therefore suggests that he pursues this matter at a later stage with a local career guidance counsellor, and provides him with names and addresses before counselling ends.

RELAPSE

Relapse needs to be addressed by both parties at the end of the counselling process. Clients must feel that their counselling needs will be met if they or their circumstances deteriorate to a point where it is difficult to cope. Clients from other cultures need particular attention because they rightly fear that there may be limited facilities that are culturally appropriate for them beyond counselling.

In fact, three of our clients did not suffer any relapse in the first year before writing this book. This is not to say that the subject was not fully discussed. Each of them was asked by the counsellor what he or she would like to do in a situation that was getting out of hand. They were able to specify circumstances under which they would need to see their counsellors again. In this way, they had more control, more choice, and were thus more confident about leaving their counsellors, than if they had not been able to discuss the subject of relapse.

Fred, however, does experience a relapse. He becomes physically ill while he is phasing out his sessions with his counsellor. He wakes up one morning with acute back pain and he panics. He calls his doctor and then his counsellor, and insists on extra sessions with her. His counsellor responds by offering an immediate appointment to discuss his fears. Fred arrives on crutches and in great distress.

> *Fred*: I feel hopeless. I feel I'm right back at square one again. Nothing I do seems to work. I don't know why I've come back; I guess I still need to talk to somebody.
>
> *Counsellor*: I'm sorry you're in so much pain today – what has your doctor said is the matter?

As Fred pours out his feelings of helplessness and futility about his future, he exclaims that counselling has achieved no change but nevertheless wants to see his counsellor more often. Fred's counsellor listens attentively and responds in a quiet and calm manner. She acknowledges his distress and pain, and checks that he has secured all the medical assistance he needs for his back. She is then free to help Fred look at his hopelessness about counselling.

> *Counsellor*: (calmly) We went through all the changes you have
> achieved on the last occasion you were here. Do you remember
> them?
> *Fred*: (reluctantly) I can just about remember.

She takes Fred through the review and the changes he has already achieved. Fred immediately responds to this by calming down and looking at his present crisis more clearly. His counsellor is then able to show him that a relapse is a good opportunity to strengthen him in ways that were not apparent earlier in the counselling process. He has the chance now to consolidate his progress and to test it against the outside world.

Towards the end of this session, Fred still wants to know if he can see her for longer. His counsellor responds by offering him one additional session, while at the same time she discusses with him the difficulties of dependency. He leaves feeling relieved.

Saying Goodbye

Saying goodbye starts long before the end of counselling. As therapeutic tasks are accomplished, counsellors will explore with their clients their feelings about endings. We have already referred to the sense of loss at the end of counselling and how to help our clients deal with this.

Saying goodbye will inevitably involve some unhappiness, as well as a sense of achievement. Counsellors share their feelings with their clients, and help them to deal constructively with these experiences. Saying goodbye is symbolic of the counselling process having been accomplished.

Transcultural counselling has been about breaking down cultural barriers and creating a safe space for change. Goodbyes do not mean that clients have resolved all their problems, but do mean that clients are ready to face their world better resourced than when they first sought counselling.

Mathilde demonstrates this process well. She attends the last appointment with her counsellor looking pensive, and there is a long silence at the start of the session.

Mathilde: I haven't anything left to say.

Counsellor: Uh-huh.

Mathilde: (long pause) I can't believe this is the last time I'm coming. I can't seem to remember what it was like before I came to see you.

Counsellor: Maybe you find it painful to look back at how you were when we started counselling.

Mathilde: Yes, but the future seems so scary. I think I've learned something from coming here, but there is still so much more to talk about. I guess I'll have to talk more to John, or my mother, or my friends. I don't want to get sick again, and I certainly don't want to come here again (laughs).

Counsellor: Okay. But are you worried that you might?

Mathilde: Yes, sometimes, but that's okay isn't it? I can still say goodbye.

Mathilde knows very well that she has only just begun some of the changes in her life that will help her with life in the UK with her husband and baby. But she has discovered resources within herself, and she has more confidence in using those around her when she isn't coping on her own. The fact that she can refer to that sense of not coping, without needing to say that she *has* to return to counselling, is itself an indication that Mathilde is ready to say goodbye.

FRIENDSHIPS AND FUTURE CONTACT

At this stage of the counselling process, the question of friendships often comes up. If the relationship between counsellor and client has been characterised by trust and warmth, our clients may want to continue seeing their counsellor socially. Counsellors too may want to maintain contact with their clients after counselling. There is much controversy about relationships between client and counsellor continuing after counselling has finished, and this issue has been addressed by the ethical guidelines of professional bodies such as the British Psychological Society, British Association for Counselling and the United Kingdom Council for Psychotherapy. A transcultural way of thinking about this takes into account the differing cultural expectations of the client, as we outline in the case of Rahima below. What matters is that counsellors are aware of their own feelings about this, and decide for themselves what, if any level of contact, is in the best interests of their clients.

For example, although *Rahima* has accepted the need for decreasing contact, she is still finding it difficult to say goodbye.

Rahima: Would you like to come round for tea next Wednesday? Now that we're finishing, I'd like to show my appreciation for all the work you've done for me.

Counsellor: Thank you for the invitation. But we've already spoken about the importance of my remaining separate from your personal life.

Rahima: (sadly) Does that mean you won't come?

Counsellor: Yes.

The counsellor refuses Rahima's invitation and explains that she feels that the counselling relationship would not benefit from this type of contact. The counsellor indicates to Rahima that the counsellor's position of relative objectivity would be jeopardised by getting involved with her client's life at a more personal level. Rahima accepts this with some sadness.

At the following session Rahima tells her counsellor that she is helping to organise a Bangladeshi Women's Festival at her local community centre. She invites her counsellor to come along and on this occasion the counsellor accepts. She is pleased to attend and gives Rahima her reasons; she has refused personal involvement but wants to affirm Rahima in her cultural context. This festival provides an ideal opportunity for this. Secondly, Rahima's counsellor is interested in and wants to increase her own knowledge of Bangladeshi culture. Lastly, she would like to be more involved with Bangladeshi members of the community.

COUNSELLORS' REVIEW

Just as clients' progress has been reviewed throughout the therapeutic process, so counsellors themselves need to assess the effects of their transcultural experience on their counselling. This is particularly important for counsellors who are members of the white majority culture. Personal review is a cyclical process. We spoke earlier in the book about beginnings and the preparations necessary for getting started in transcultural counselling. Reviewing the past is itself a preparation for the next counselling relationship.

Counsellors need to assess changes that have occurred within themselves since the beginning of the counselling process. Let's look at

Clifford's counsellor. She started counselling by feeling somewhat over-whelmed by his varied needs. She tackled these feelings by finding out more about his culture before she offered him any help. She went to her local library and the Commonwealth Institute in London, for factual as well as cultural information about Nigeria. The effect of establishing this information was to start to break down barriers between herself and Clifford, and eventually to build trust.

In reviewing her progress, the counsellor sees that she had expected too much of Clifford as a result of *her* initial enthusiasm. Her search for cultural knowledge is a necessary first step to her growth. But more than this is required of the counsellor. The prejudice and racism in Clifford's world cannot be dissipated by factual information alone; she realises that trust takes patience and consistent sensitivity to cultural issues.

She also expected too much of herself at the beginning of counselling. Factual information alone cannot break down her own racial stereotypes and assumptions about Clifford. In reviewing changes, the counsellor reflects on Clifford's feedback about her non-verbal behaviour, and accommodates it within her personal style of counselling. She has become more comfortable with Clifford's proximity and need for more sponta-neous facial expressions. She feels more confident and is less likely to feel daunted by other referrals outside her own culture.

ALTERNATIVE RESOURCES

Clients from other cultures have often had to seek help from resources set up by their own communities before finding counselling. It is to these resources that the clients will return after counselling, together with family, friends, neighbours and local public services. Community resources are culturally appropriate but may not be funded or staffed for counselling purposes. In one directory (Ward, 1986), 300 groups offering a service to people with mental health problems in London were con-tacted. Only ten of these had any trained or specialist workers; these agencies were providing a mental health service out of sheer necessity.

Clients who have had effective transcultural counselling will, however, be able to return to and use community resources in a different way. Clients can now help visit these groups for support, contact and self-help, rather than for crisis intervention or deep personal conflict.

In summary, we have endeavoured to show that task assessment, feed-back, review, decreasing contact with clients and saying goodbye are all part of the process of preparing clients for endings. We have explained the importance of ending counselling with clients from other cultures in a well-planned and sensitive way, and some of the consequences of neglecting these issues. We have discussed the significance of loss and separation for both parties, and what preparation needs to be made for possible relapse.

CONCLUSION

We have tried to show throughout this book that a transcultural approach is an enrichment of *all* counselling practice. We have shared our mistakes as well as our successes with four clients in order to give practical examples of this approach. Some of our suggestions have been based upon what other writers have described but, on the whole, we have used our own working experiences. We have often opted for pragmatic ways of dealing with transcultural issues. However, our underlying philosophy is based on the belief that cultural and racial understanding are an essential requirement for counsellors approaching the twenty-first century.

REFERENCES

Ahmad W.I.U. (ed.) (1993) *'Race' and Health in Contemporary Britain.* Buckingham: Open University Press.

Alston, M.H., Small, E.B. and Whiteside, M.D. (1992) 'Loneliness in Black Elderly', *Journal of National Black Nurses Association*, 5(2): 37–44.

Argyle, M. (ed.) (1981) *Social Skills and Health.* London: Methuen.

Baker, F.M. (1994) 'Psychiatric Treatment of Older African Americans', *Hospital and Community Psychiatry*, 45(1): 32–7.

Bavington, J. and A. Majid (1986) 'Psychiatric Services for Ethnic Minority Groups', in J. Cox (ed.), *Transcultural Psychiatry.* London: Croom Helm.

Bennett, E., Dennis, M., Dosanjh, N., Mahtani, A., Miller, A., Nadirshaw, Z. and Patel, N. (1995) *Resource Pack for Trainers: Clinical Psychology, 'Race' and Culture: Introductory Module.* Clinical Psychology, 'Race' and Culture Special Interest Group, British Psychological Society.

Benyon, J. (1984) *Scarman and After.* Oxford: Pergamon Press.

Bhatt, C. (1991) *AIDS & The Black Communities.* London: BHAN Policy Report 1.

Bhavnani, K., and Haraway, D. (1994) Shifting Identities Shifting Racisms: An Introduction, *Feminism and Psychology*, 4(1): 5–18.

Bhopal, R. (1997) 'Is research into Ethnicity and Health Racist, Unsound, or Important Science?', *British Medical Journal*, 314, 1751–6.

Blair, W., A. Khera, S. Khoot and R. Patel (1981) 'Level Crossing?', in J. Cheetham, W. James, M. Loney, B. Mayor and W. Prescott (eds), *Social and Community Work in a Multiracial Society.* London: Harper and Row.

Bracken, P. (1998) 'Hidden Agenda: Deconstructing Post Traumatic Stress Disorder', in P.J. Bracken and C. Petty (eds), *Rethinking the Trauma of War.* London: Free Association Books.

British Association for Counselling (1977) *Invitation to Membership.* BAC, 37a Sheep Street, Rugby, Warwickshire, CV21 3BX, UK.

British Association for Counselling (1985) *Counselling: Definition of small Terms in use with Expansion and Rationale.* Rugby: BAC.

Brown, C. (1984) *Black and White Britain: The Third PSI Survey.* London: Gower.

Burke, A. (1986). 'Racism, Prejudice and Mental illness', in J. Cox (ed.), *Transcultural Psychiatry.* London: Croom Helm.

Butcher, J., Nezami, E., and Exner, J. (1998) 'Psychological Assessments of People in Diverse Cultures', in S.S. Kazarian and D.R. Evans (eds), *Cultural Clinical Psychology: Theory Research and Practice.* Oxford: Oxford University Press.

Chaplin, J. (1999) *Feminist Counselling in Action*, 2nd edn. London: Sage Publications.

Cheetham, J. (1972) *Social Work with Immigrants.* London: Routledge and Kegan Paul.

Cheetham, J. (1981) 'Social Services in the Community: Introduction', in J. Cheetham, W. James, M. Loney, B. Mayor and W. Prescott (eds), *Social and Community Work in a Multiracial Society.* London: Harper and Row.

Cheetham, J. (1982) 'Client Groups, Some Priorities', in J. Cheetham (ed.), *Social Work and Ethnicity.* London: George Allen and Unwin.

Clarkson, P. and Nippoda, Y. (1998) 'Cross-cultural Issues in Counselling Psychology Practice: a Qualitative Study of one Multicultural Training Organisation', in P. Clarkson (ed.), *Counselling Psychology: Integrating Theory, Research and Supervised Practice.* London: Routledge.

Cochrane, R. (1979) 'Psychological and Behavioural Disturbance in West Indians, Indians and Pakistanis in Britain: A Comparison of Rates among Children and Adults', *British Journal of Psychiatry,* 134: 201–10.

Cochrane, R., and Bal, S.S. (1989) Mental Hospital Admission Rates of Immigrants to England: A Comparison of 1971 and 1981, *Social Psychiatry and Psychiatric Epidemiology,* 24: 2–11.

Cox, J. (ed.) (1986) *Transcultural Psychiatry.* London: Croom Helm.

CVS (1997) *Ethnicity and Disability: Moving towards Equity in Service Provision.* London: CVS Consultants.

d'Ardenne, P. (1986a), 'Transcultural Differences Affecting Personal Problems', in R. France and M. Robson, *Behaviour Therapy in Primary Care: A Practical Guide.* London: Croom Helm.

d'Ardenne, P. (1986b) 'Sexual Dysfunction in a Transcultural Setting: Assessment, Treatment and Research', *Sexual and Marital Therapy,* 1(1): 23–34.

d'Ardenne, P. (1988) 'Transcultural Sexual Problems', in M. Cole and W. Dryden (eds), *Sex Therapy in Britain Today.* Milton Keynes: Open University Press.

d'Ardenne, P. (1996) 'Sexual Health for Men in Culturally Diverse Communities – some psychological considerations', *Sexual and Marital Therapy*, 11(3): 289–96.

Dominelli, L. (1988) *Anti-Racist Social Work.* London: Macmillan Education.

Durrant, J. (1986) 'Racism and the Under-Fives', in V. Coombe and A. Little (eds), *Race and Social Work.* London: Tavistock Publications.

Eleftheriadou, Z. (1994) *Transcultural Counselling.* London: Central Book Publishing Ltd.

Fatimilehin, I.A. and Coleman, P.G. (1998) 'Appropriate Services for African-Caribbean Families: Views from one Community', *Clinical Psychology Forum*, 111: 6–11.

Fernando, S. (1986) 'Depression in Ethnic Minorities', in J. Cox (ed.), *Transcultural Psychiatry.* London: Croom Helm.

Fernando, S. (1988) *Race and Culture in Psychiatry.* London: Croom Helm.

Fernando, S. (1991) *Mental Health, Race and Culture.* London: Macmillan Mind Publications.

Fernando, S. (1995) 'Social Realities and Mental Health', in S. Fernando, (ed.), *Mental Health in a Multi-ethnic Society: A Multi-disciplinary Handbook.* London: Routledge.

Furnham, A. and S. Bochner (1986) *Culture Shock: Psychological Reactions to Unfamiliar Environments.* London: Methuen.

Gilbert, M. and Shmukler, D. (1996) 'Counselling Psychology in Groups', in R. Woolfe and W. Dryden (eds), *Handbook of Counselling Psychology.* London: Sage.

Gordon, P. and F. Klug (1984) *Racism and Discrimination in Britain.* London: The Runnymede Trust.

Gorst-Unsworth, C. and Goldenberg, E. (1998), 'Psychological Sequel of Torture and Organised Violence Suffered by Refugees From Iraq', *British Journal of Psychiatry*, 172: 90–4.

Harrison, G., Owens, D., Holton, A., Neilson, D. and Boot, D. (1988) 'A Prospective Study of Severe Mental Disorder in Afro-Caribbean Patients', *Psychological Medicine*, 18: 643–57.

Henley, A . (1979) *Asian Patients in Hospitals and at Home.* London: King Edward's Hospital Fund.

Holland, S. (1995) 'Interaction in Women's Mental Health and Neighbourhood Development', in S. Fernando (ed.), *Mental Health in a Multi-ethnic Society: A Multi-disciplinary Handbook.* London: Routledge.

Husband, C. (1986) 'Racism, Prejudice and Social Policy', in V. Coombe and A. Little (eds), *Race and Social Work*. London: Tavistock Publications.

Jacobs, M. (1988) *Psychodynamic Counselling in Action*. London: Sage Publications.

Jaranson, J.J. and Bamford, P. (1987) *Program Models for Mental Health Treatment of Refugees* (NIMH Contract No. 278-85-0024). St Paul, MN: University of Minnesota, Refugee Assistance Program – Mental Health Technical Assistance Center.

Jenkins, S. and M. Sauber (1988) 'Ethnic Associations in New York and Services to Immigrants', in S. Jenkins (ed.), *Ethnic Associations to Immigrants in Five Countries*. New York: Columbia University Press.

Jensen, A.R. (1981) *Straight Talk About Mental Tests*. London: Methuen.

John, G. (1981) 'Black Self-help Projects', in J. Cheetham, W. James, H. Loney, B. Mayor and W. Prescott (eds), *Social and Community Work in a Multiracial Society*. London: Harper and Row.

Kareem, J. (1992) 'The Nafsiyat Intercultural Therapy Centre: Ideas and Experience in Intercultural Therapy', in J. Kareem and R. Littlewood, (eds), *Intercultural Therapy: Themes, Interpretations and Practice*. Oxford: Blackwell Scientific Publications.

Kareem, J. and Littlewood, R. (eds) (1992) *Intercultural Therapy: Themes, Interpretations and Practice*. Oxford: Blackwell Scientific Publications.

Katz, J.H. (1978) *White Awareness: Handbook for Anti-racism Training*. Norman and London: University of Oklahoma Press.

Katz, J.H. (1985) 'The Sociopolitical Nature of Counselling', *The Counselling Psychologist,* 13(4): 615–24.

King, M., Coker, E., Leavey, G., Hoare, A. and Johnson-Sabine, E. (1994) 'Incidence of Psychotic Illness in London: Comparison of Ethnic Groups, *British Medical Journal*, 309: 1115–19.

Krause, I.-B. (1989) 'Sinking Heart: A Punjabi Communication of Distress', *Social Science and Medicine*, 29(4): 563–75.

Krause, I.-B. (1998) *Therapy Across Cultures*. London: Sage Publications.

Lago, C. and Thompson, J. (1989) 'Counselling and Race', in W. Dryden, D. Charles-Edwards and R. Wolfe (eds), *Handbook of Counselling in Britain*. London: Tavistock-Routledge.

Lago, C. and Thompson, J. (1996) *Race, Culture and Counselling*. Buckingham: Open University Press.

Leininger, M. (1985) 'Transcultural Caring: A Different Way to Help People', in P. Pedersen (ed.), *Handbook of Cross-cultural Counseling and Therapy*. Westport: Greenwood Press.

Littlewood, R. (1992) 'Psychiatric Diagnosis and Racial Bias: Empirical and Interpretive Approaches', *Social Science and Medicine*, 34(2): 141–9.

Littlewood, R. and M. Lipsedge (1982) *Aliens and Alienists: Ethnic Minorities and Psychiatry.* Harmondsworth: Penguin.

Littlewood, R. and Lipsedge, M. (1988) 'Psychiatric Illness among British Afro-Caribbeans', *British Medical Journal*, 29: 950–51.

Littlewood, R. and Lipsedge, M. (1997) *Aliens and Alienists: Ethnic Minorities and Psychiatry.* 3rd edition. London: Unwin Hyman.

Lonner, W.J. and N.D. Sondberg (1985) 'Assessment in Cross-cultural Counseling and Therapy', in P. Pedersen (ed.), *Handbook of Cross-cultural Counseling and Therapy.* Westport: Greenwood Press.

Lorion, R.P. and D.L. Parron (1985) 'Countering the Countertransference: A Strategy for Treating the Untreatable', in P. Pedersen (ed.), *Handbook of Cross-cultural Counseling and Therapy.* Westport: Greenwood Press.

MacCarthy, B. (1988) 'Clinical Work with Ethnic Minorities', in F. Watts (ed.), *New Developments in Clinical Psychology Volume 2.* British Psychological Society. Chichester: John Wiley and Sons.

MacCarthy, B. and Craissati, J. (1989) 'Ethnic Differences in Response to Adversity', *Social Psychiatry and Psychiatric Epidemiology*, 24: 196–201.

McGovern, D. and Cope, R. (1987) 'First Psychiatric Admission Rates of First and Second Generation Afro-Caribbeans', *Social Psychiatry*, 22: 139–49.

Mahtani, A. and Huq, A.H. (1993) 'The Use of a Western Model Across Cultures', *British Journal of Guidance and Counselling*, 21(1): 35–40.

Mahtani, A. and Marks, L. (1994) 'Developing a Primary Care Service that is Racially and Culturally appropriate', *Clinical Psychology Forum*, 65: 27–31.

Maternity Services Liaison Scheme (1984) *Annual Report.* Montefiore Centre, Deal Street, London, E1.

Mearns, D. and B. Thorne (1988) *Person-centred Counselling in Action.* London: Sage Publications.

Miller, A.C. and Thomas, L. (1994) 'Introducing Ideas about Racism and Culture into Family Therapy Training', *Context*, 20, autumn: 25–9.

Milner, D. (1983) *Children and Race: Ten Years On.* London: Ward Lock International.

Modood, T., Berthoud, R., Lakey, J., Nazroo, J., Smith, P., Virdee, S., and Beishon, S., (1997) *Ethnic Minorities in Britain: Diversity and Disadvantage.* London: Policy Studies Institute.

Moorhouse, S. (1992) 'Quantitative Research in Intercultural Therapy: Some Methodological Considerations', in J. Kareem and R. Littlewood, (eds), *Intercultural Therapy: Themes, Interpretations and Practice.* Oxford: Blackwell Scientific Publications.

132

Morris, J. (1991) *Pride Against Prejudice: Transforming Attitudes to Disability*. London: The Women's Press.

Mullick, Y. and Baker, M. (1998) 'Arranged Marriage and Own Choice Marriage: A Rationale for Both Types of Marriage Amongst Second-generation Asian Women', *Clinical Psychology Forum*, 118: 33–6.

Murphy, H. (1986) 'The Mental Health Impact of British Cultural Traditions', in J. Cox (ed.), *Transcultural Psychiatry*. London: Croom Helm.

Nadirshaw, Z. (1997) 'Cultural Issues', in J. O'Hara and A. Sperlinger (eds), *Adults with Learning Disabilities*, Chichester: John Wiley and Sons.

Nadirshaw, Z. (1998) 'Contemporary Issues in Clinical Psychology Service Provision', in K. Bhui and D.W.B. Olajide (eds), *Cross-cultural Mental Health Care*, London: Saunders.

NAFSIYAT (1985) *Annual Report*. 278 Seven Sisters Road, London N4 2HY.

Nazroo, J.Y. (1997) *Ethnicity and Mental Health: Findings from a National Community Survey*. London. Policy Studies Institute.

Nelson-Jones, R. (1988) *Practical Counselling and Helping Skills*. London: Cassell.

Newland, J. (1998) 'Editorial: Race and Culture', Special Issue, *Clinical Psychology Forum*, 118: 5.

Nicolson, P. (1992) 'Gender Issues in the Organisation of Clinical Psychology', in J. Ussher and P. Nicolson (eds), *Gender Issues in Clinical Psychology*. London: Routledge.

Oliver, M. (1990) *The Politics of Disablement*. Basingstoke: Macmillan Education.

Parkes, C.M. (1986) *Bereavement: Studies of Grief in Adult Life*. London and New York: Tavistock Publications.

Patel, N. (1992) 'Psychological Disturbance, Social Support and Stressors: A Community Survey of Immigrant Asian Women and the Indigenous Population', *Counselling Psychology Quarterly*, 5(3): 263–76.

Pedersen, P. (1985) 'Intercultural Criteria for Mental-health Training' in P. Pedersen (ed.), *Handbook of Cross-cultural Counseling and Therapy*. Westport: Greenwood Press.

Pedersen, P. (1988) *A Handbook for Developing Multicultural Awareness*. Alexandria: American Association for Counseling and Development.

Pedersen, P.B., Draguns, J.G., Lonner, W.J. and Trimble, J.E. (1996) *Counseling Across Cultures*. 4th edition, Thousand Oaks: Sage.

Phillips, D. and T. Rathwell (1986) 'Ethnicity and Health: Introduction and Definitions', in D. Phillips and T. Rathwell (eds), *Health, Race and Ethnicity*. London: Croom Helm.

Phoenix, A. (1997) 'The Place of "Race" and Ethnicity in the Lives of Children and Young People, *Educational and Child Psychology*, 14(3): 5–24.

Rack, P. (1982) *Race, Culture and Mental Disorder*. London and New York: Tavistock Publications.

Reber, A. (1985) *Dictionary of Psychology*. Harmondsworth: Penguin.

Richman, N. (1998) 'Looking Before and After: Refugees and Asylum Seekers in the West', in P.J. Bracken and C. Petty (eds), *Rethinking the Trauma of War*. London: Free Association Books.

Richmond, J. (1986) 'The Language of Black Children and the Language Debate in Schools', in D. Sutcliffe and A. Wong (eds), *The Language of the Black Experience*. Oxford: Basil Blackwell.

Rogers, C.R. (1951) *Client-centred Therapy*. London: Constable.

Romero, D. (1985) 'Cross-cultural Counselling: Brief Reactions for the Practitioner', *The Counselling Psychologist*, 13(4): 665–71.

Roth, A. and Fonagy, P. (1996) *What Works for Whom? A Critical Review of Psychotherapy Research*. London: The Guilford Press.

Rushton, J.P. (1990) 'Race Differences, R/K Theory, and a Reply to Flynn', *The Psychologist*, 5: 195–8.

Sashidharan, S.P. (1986) 'Ideology and Politics in Transcultural Psychiatry', in J. Cox (ed.), *Transcultural Psychiatry*. London: Croom Helm.

Sashidharan, S.P. (1993) 'Afro-Caribbeans and Schizophrenia: The Ethnic Vulnerability Re-examined', *International Review of Psychiatry*, 5: 129–44.

Sashidharan, S.P. and Francis, E. (1993) 'Epidemiology, ethnicity and schizophrenia', in W.I.U. Ahmad (ed.), *'Race' and Health in Contemporary Britain*. Buckingham: Open University Press.

Shackman, J. (1984) *A Handbook on Working with, Employing and Training Interpreters*. Cambridge: National Extension College.

Shillito-Clarke, C. (1996) 'Ethical Issues in Counselling Psychology', in R. Wolfe and W. Dryden (eds), *Handbook of Counselling Psychology*. London: Sage.

Sinclair, J.M. (1995) *Collins Concise Dictionary*. 3rd edition. Glasgow: HarperCollins.

Smith, E.M.J. (1985a) 'Counseling Black Women', in P. Pedersen (ed.), *Handbook of Cross-cultural Counseling and Therapy*. Westport: Greenwood Press.

Smith, E.M.J. (1985b) 'Ethnic Minorities: Life Stress, Social Support and Mental Health Issues', *The Counseling Psychologist*, 13(4): 537–79.

Sommerfield, P. (1979) 'The Black Social Workers' Project', in M. Marshall, G. Mitchell and A. Sackville (eds), *Social Work in Action*. Birmingham: British Association of Social Work.

Sue, D.W. (1981) *Counseling the Culturally Different: Theory and Practice*. New York: John Wiley and Sons.

Sue, D.W. and Sue, D. (1990) *Counseling the Culturally Different: Theory and Practice.* 2nd edition. New York: John Wiley and Sons.

Sue, D.W., Arredondo, P. and McDavis, R.J. (1992) 'Multicultural Counseling Competencies and Standards: A Call to the Profession,' *Journal of Counseling and Development*, 70: 477–86.

Summerfield, D. (1998) 'The Social Experience of War and Some Issues for the Humanitarian Field', in P.J. Bracken and C. Petty (eds), *Rethinking the Trauma of War.* London: Free Association Books.

Swain, J., Finkelstein, V., French, S. and Oliver, M. (eds) (1994) *Disabling Barriers – Enabling Environments.* London: Sage.

Thomas, L. (1992) 'Racism and Psychotherapy: Working with racism in the Consulting Room – an Analytical View', in J. Kareem and R. Littlewood (eds), *Intercultural Therapy: Themes, Interpretations and Practice.* Oxford. Blackwell Scientific Publications.

Thomas, T. and S. Sillen (1972) *Racism and Psychiatry.* Secaucus: The Citadel Press.

Tizard, B. and Phoenix, A. (1995) 'The Identity of Mixed Parentage Adolescents', *Journal of Child Psychology & Psychiatry & Allied Disciplines*, 36 (8): 1399–410.

Triandis, H. (1980) 'Introduction', in H. Triandis and W. Lambert (eds), *Handbook of Cross-cultural Psychology, Volume 1.* Boston: Allyn and Bacon.

Triandis, H. (1985) 'Some Major Dimensions of Cultural Variation in Client Populations', in P. Pedersen (ed.), *Handbook of Cross-cultural Counseling and Therapy.* Westport: Greenwood Press.

Triseliotis, J. (1986) 'Transcultural Social Work', in J. Cox (ed.), *Transcultural Psychiatry.* London: Croom Helm.

Truax, C.B. and R.R. Carkhuff (1967) *Towards Effective Counseling and Psychotherapy: Training and Practice.* Chicago: Aldine.

Ussher, J.M. and Nicolson, P. (eds) (1992) *Gender Issues in Clinical Psychology.* London: Routledge.

Van der Veer, G. (1992) *Counselling and Therapy with Refugees.* Chichester: John Wiley and Sons.

Virdee, S. (1997) 'Racial Harassment', in T. Modood, R. Berthoud, J. Lakey, J. Nazroo, P. Smith, S. Virdee and S. Beishon (eds), *Ethnic Minorities in Britain: Diversity and Disadvantage.* London: Policy Studies Institute.

Wallbank, S. (1997) 'Counselling in Voluntary Organizations', in S. Palmer and G. McMahon (eds), *Handbook of Counselling.* 2nd edition. London: Routledge.

Wallis, S. (1981) 'Bengali Families in Camden', in J. Cheetham, W. James, M.

Loney, B. Mayor and W. Prescott (eds), *Social and Community Work in a Multiracial Society.* London: Harper and Row.

Ward, L. (1986) *Directory of Black and Ethnic Community Mental Health Services in London: Voluntary Sector.* London: MIND South East.

Ward, L. (1993) 'Race Equality and Employment in the National Health Service', in W.I.U. Ahmad (ed.), *'Race' and Health in Contemporary Britain.* Buckingham: Open University Press.

Washington, M.H. (ed.) (1980) *Any Woman's Blues.* London: Virago.

Watson, G. and Williams, J. (1992) 'Feminist Practice in Therapy', in J.M. Ussher and P. Nicolson (eds), *Gender Issues in Clinical Psychology.* London: Routledge.

Webb-Johnson, A. (1991) *A Cry for Change: An Asian Perspective on Developing Quality Health Care.* London: Confederation of Indian Organisations.

Winter, K.A. and Young, M.Y. (1998) 'Biopsychosocial Considerations in Refugee Mental Health', in S.S. Kazarian and D.R. Evans (eds), *Cultural Clinical Psychology: Theory, Research and Practice.* Oxford: Oxford University Press.

Wong, A. (1986) 'Creole as a Language of Power and Solidarity', in D. Sutcliffe and A. Wong (eds), *The Language of Black Experience.* Oxford: Basil Blackwell.

Wright, J. (1993) 'African-American Male Sexual Behavior and the Risk of HIV Infection', *Human Organisation*, 52: 431–3.

INDEX

Celebrating
20 Years
of
Counselling in Action

SAGE Counselling in Action Series
www.sagepub.co.uk/counselling

Person-Centred
Counselling in Action
3rd Edition

Dave Mearns and Brian Thorne

978-1-4129-2855-7

Standards and Ethics for
Counselling in Action
2nd Edition

Tim Bond

978-0-7619-6309-7

Psychodynamic
Counselling in Action
3rd Edition

Michael Jacobs

978-1-4129-0215-1

Integrative Counselling
Skills in Action
2nd Edition

Sue Culley and Tim Bond

978-0-7619-6994-5

Cognitive-Behavioural
Counselling in Action

Peter Trower, Andrew Casey and Windy Dryden

978-0-8039-8048-8

Key Issues for
Counselling in Action
2nd Edition

ed by Windy Dryden and Andrew Reeves

978-1-4129-4699-5

Transactional Analysis
Counselling in Action
3rd Edition

Ian Stewart

978-1-4129-3495-4

Gestalt
Counselling in Action
3rd Edition

Petrūska Clarkson

978-1-4129-0085-0

Rational Emotive Behavioural
Counselling in Action
3rd Edition

Windy Dryden and Michael Neenan

978-1-4129-0213-7

Transcultural
Counselling in Action
2nd Edition

Patricia d'Ardenne and Aruna Mahtani

978-0-7619-6315-8